CAMBRIDGE
UNIVERSITY PRESS

UNIVERSITY *of* CAMBRIDGE
ESOL Examinations

Cambridge English

Compact
First for Schools

Student's Book

Barbara Thomas
Laura Matthews

CAMBRIDGE UNIVERSITY PRESS
Cambridge, New York, Melbourne, Madrid, Cape Town,
Singapore, São Paulo, Delhi, Mexico City

Cambridge University Press
The Edinburgh Building, Cambridge CB2 8RU, UK

www.cambridge.org
Information on this title: www.cambridge.org/9781107603974

First published 2013

Printed in Italy by L.E.G.O. S.p.A.

A catalogue record for this publication is available from the British Library

ISBN 978-1-107-60397-4 Student's Book without answers with CD-ROM
ISBN 978-1-107-60400-1 Teacher's Book
ISBN 978-1-107-60398-1 Workbook without answers with Audio CD
ISBN 978-1-107-60401-8 Student's Pack
ISBN 978-1-107-60399-8 Class Audio CD

CONTENTS

MAP OF THE UNITS

Unit	Topics	Grammar	Vocabulary	Reading
1 Family and friends	Family celebrations Friends	Present and future tenses State verbs Comparisons	Words often confused Matching expressions with similar meanings	Part 1: multiple-choice questions + long text
2 Exploring the world	Adventure and travel Where you live	Past tenses Prepositions of time Adverb formation	Word building (1): adjective suffixes (-able, -al, -ous) Cities, towns and villages	Part 2: gapped text
3 The entertainment industry	Films Music	Linking words and phrases The passive	Film and cinema Music	Part 3: multiple-matching
4 Active life	Sports Keeping fit and healthy	Modal verbs Prepositions following verbs and adjectives	Sports Food Word building (2): noun suffixes (-ence, -ity, -(s/t)ion)	Part 1: multiple-choice questions + long text
5 Learning	Ambitions and achievements Education	Conditionals	Phrasal verbs School subjects and education Careers Education	Part 3: multiple-matching
6 Natural world	Environment and weather Wildlife	Countable and uncountable nouns Articles so and such (a/an), too and enough	Natural environment and weather Environmental problems Wildlife	Part 2: gapped text
7 People and style	Shopping and fashion People and feelings	Verbs and expressions followed by to-infinitive or -ing form Reported speech	Clothes Shopping Feelings	Part 1: multiple-choice questions + long text
8 Keeping up to date	Science Technology	Relative clauses	Science Computers Word building (3): prefixes and suffixes	Part 3: multiple-matching

Writing	Use of English	Listening	Speaking
Part 1 email: responding appropriately, commenting, giving opinions, suggesting and apologising	Part 1: multiple-choice cloze	Part 3: multiple-matching	Part 1: leisure activities Part 2: comparing ways of spending free time
Part 2 story: sequencing, using adjectives and adverbs	Part 2: open cloze Part 3: word formation	Part 1: multiple-choice questions + short texts	Part 3: discussing preferences, agreeing and disagreeing Part 4: talking about where you live
Part 2 review: organising paragraphs, linking words and phrases	Part 4: key word transformations	Part 4: multiple-choice questions + long text	Part 1: adding extra information and comments Part 2: talking about films and music, avoiding unknown words, giving preferences
Part 1 letter: writing formally and informally	Part 2: open cloze Part 3: word formation	Part 2: sentence completion	Part 3: asking for opinions and reacting to opinions Part 4: discussing sports and keeping fit
Part 2 report: formal and informal language, making recommendations	Part 1: multiple-choice cloze Part 4: key word transformations	Part 2: sentence completion	Part 1: discussing ambitions, achievements and education Part 2: making guesses
Part 2 article: keeping the reader's attention, formal and informal styles, introductions and endings	Part 2: open cloze	Part 4: multiple-choice questions + long text	Part 3: agreeing, disagreeing, making a comment or suggestion Part 4: discussing ways of helping the environment
Part 2 informal letter: linking words and phrases, describing a person	Part 4: key word transformations	Part 3: multiple-matching	Part 1: expressing likes and dislikes Part 2: comparing different ways of shopping
Part 2 essay: planning an essay, using a range of vocabulary	Part 3: word formation	Part 1: multiple-choice questions + short texts	Part 3: structuring a conversation Part 4: discussing technology

Family and friends
LISTENING Family celebrations

Part 3

1 Look at the photos, which all show families getting together. Is everybody enjoying themselves? Why do you think they are spending time together?

2 Work in pairs. Talk about family celebrations. What do you celebrate with your family? How do you celebrate? Which celebrations do you like best?

3 🔘 1.02 Listen to Emily talking about a family celebration. Answer these questions.

1 What usually happens? Is it usually well organised?
2 Was there a change of plan this year? Did everything go well?
3 Did anyone disagree with the plan?

4 🔘 1.02 Listen again. What does Emily say about her family's celebration? Choose one answer from A–E. Your answers in Exercise 3 will help you.

A It was less well organised than usual.
B There was an unexpected event on the day.
C It lasted longer than usual.
D There was a difference of opinion.
E A change of plan was successful.

> **Exam tip**
> The question may test a detail or a large part of what you hear. Listen for the general meaning as well as checking the details against the questions. ✓

Exam task

> The task below is shorter than in the exam. In Listening Part 3 you hear five speakers and match them with six possible statements. You have already heard Emily. Now you will hear three more people.

🔘 1.03 You will hear three people talking about a family celebration. Choose from the list A–E what each speaker says about the celebration.

A It was less well organised than usual.
B There was an unexpected event on the day.
C It lasted longer than usual.
D There was a difference of opinion.
E A change of plan was successful.

Speaker 1 .....
Speaker 2 .....
Speaker 3 .....

> **Exam tip**
> In the exam, you will hear each recording twice. ✓

USE OF ENGLISH

Part 1

Vocabulary – Words often confused

1 ○ Work in pairs. Complete the sentences with the correct word or expression.

> **Exam tip**
>
> This part of the exam tests mainly vocabulary but some questions will test grammar too. ✓

1 Here are some fixed expressions with *at*. Check the meaning of each phrase in each gap and then choose the correct expression.

> at all   at last   at least   at once

A Most of my friends have .... one computer in their homes.

B I got into bed and I was so tired I fell asleep ....

C I waited for my friend for ages and .... she arrived.

D She didn't know her grandfather .... because he never visited.

2 Sometimes you need to look at the meaning of the word and also the grammar. Choose the correct word for each gap.

> believes   demands   depends   expects

A Our teacher .... us to speak English in her lessons.

B Playing chess .... a lot of concentration.

C My granny .... on us to get all her shopping for her.

D My father .... in letting me make my own decisions.

2 Quickly read the text in the Exam task. Answer these questions.

1 What is significant about 21 December in the most northern / most southern places?

2 What do people celebrate in northern countries in the middle of December?

Exam task

> In Use of English Part 1 you read a text with 12 gaps and an example. The text below has nine gaps and an example.

For questions 1–9, read the text below and decide which answer (A, B, C or D) best fits each gap. There is an example at the beginning (0).

Winter celebrations

In the countries which are furthest north and south on earth, the (0) ...A... of light varies (1) .... between winter and summer. In the northern hemisphere the shortest day is on or about 21 December. In (2) .... fact, in some places there is no daylight at (3) .... during the day in the middle of winter. In the southern hemisphere it is the opposite, of course, and 21 December is the longest day.

Throughout history, people in (4) .... every northern country have (5) .... traditions to celebrate the fact that the days would (6) .... both lighter and longer after the middle of December. From then onwards, people would wait impatiently for the return of the sun, which they (7) .... on. They were hunters so the seasons and the weather (8) .... a very important part in their lives. Food was in short supply in winter months so a whole community would share meals during the darkest days. They lit fires and candles and sang and danced. Some of the traditions (9) .... to this day.

0	A amount	B number	C total	D size
1	A extremely	B highly	C hugely	D terribly
2	A genuine	B actual	C true	D real
3	A least	B once	C last	D all
4	A about	B virtually	C approximately	D quite
5	A expanded	B advanced	C progressed	D developed
6	A increase	B happen	C get	D change
7	A depended	B demanded	C believed	D expected
8	A made	B played	C produced	D involved
9	A survive	B support	C keep	D maintain

3 Read the text again and check your answers. Does each one fit the meaning?

1 SPEAKING   Friends

Part 1

1 ⊙ **1.04** Look at the Speaking Part 1 questions and the possible answers in the table below. Listen to George and Francesca answering the questions. Note down the extra information they add.

Question	Answer	Extra information
1 Do you do any activities after school?	diving	
2 When do you do your homework?	after dinner	
3 What do you usually do at the weekend?	friends, grandmother	
4 What are you going to do next weekend?	friends, cinema, guitar	

2 ⊙ **1.04** Complete these sentences from the recording. Listen again if you need to.

1 I .... to dive.
2 When I .... home from school, I .... TV.
3 I .... the bus to town.
4 We .... to the cinema.
5 I .... my guitar most of the day.
6 I .... in a concert next Tuesday.

Grammar – Present and future tenses

3 Work in pairs. Look at the tenses George and Francesca use to talk about the present and future.

1 Which tense does George use when he talks about diving?
2 Which tense does he use for the things he does regularly?
3 Francesca uses two different tenses to talk about next Saturday. Why?
4 Why does she use a continuous tense to talk about playing the guitar on Sunday?
5 Which tense does she use to talk about the concert? Is it definitely happening?

4 Look at the sentences in A and B below. Which is correct, A or B?

A
I like to relax.
I prefer to do my homework after dinner.
I know I need to practise.

B
I'm liking to relax.
I'm preferring to do my homework after dinner.
I'm knowing I need to practise.

What do you notice about the verbs *like*, *prefer* and *know*? Can you think of other verbs which behave in the same way?

5 ⊙ Choose the correct answer.

1 Amy, can I change the time that we *meet* / *'re meeting* tomorrow?
2 I *want* / *'m wanting* to visit you soon.
3 I *normally spend* / *'m normally spending* most of July at the seaside.
4 Next Saturday we *go* / *'re going* to a Greek restaurant.
5 I *'m thinking* / *think* it is a good idea to go camping.
6 We will be very tired when we *get* / *'ll get* home.
7 Tomorrow I can't come to school because I *'ll go* / *'m going* to the dentist.
8 I'll do my homework in the morning before I *'ll go* / *go* to school.
9 I *write* / *'m writing* this note to tell you that I *'m going to miss* / *'m missing* tomorrow's class.
10 I'm really happy that you *come* / *'re coming* to Italy.

G *See page 78*

Exam task

Now work with a partner and ask and answer the questions in Exercise 1.

Exam tip

You will get more marks if you add some detail. Think about why, when and how you do things to expand your answers. ✓

Part 2

6 Look at the first two photographs. Which of the following adjectives, verbs, nouns and expressions could you use to talk about them?

bored ☐   energetic ☐   crowded ☐
excited ☐   lazy ☐

chat ☐   concentrate ☐   relax ☐

countryside ☐   exercise ☐

in the distance ☐   indoors ☐   outdoors ☐
a quiet spot ☐   fresh air ☐   in the shade ☐

7 Think of the advantages of spending your time like the people in these two photographs.

8 Look at the script your teacher gives you. Does Francesca give the same advantages as you?

Grammar – Comparisons

9 These sentences make comparisons with different adjectives and nouns. Put the words in *italics* in the correct order.

1 The people in the first photo *happier / than / seem / much* the people in the second photo.
2 The people in the second photo are indoors, which *enjoyable / being / as / isn't / as* in the fresh air.
3 They *getting / exercise / probably / more / are /.*
4 They *than / energetic / are / more* the people in the first photo.
5 They *less / than / will / money / spend* going to the gym.

10 Look at the other two photos above. Write two or three sentences comparing them, using some of these words.

| expensive | far more | fun |
| interesting | much less | thrilling |

G *See page 78*

Exam task

Work in pairs. Choose two of the photographs each. Take turns to talk about your photographs. Time yourselves. Try to talk for about one minute each.

> The photographs show people spending their free time in different ways. Compare the photographs and answer this question.
> • What are the advantages for the people of spending their time in these ways?

Exam tip

A question you have to answer is printed above the photographs in the exam. Make sure you answer this question when you are talking.

When you have finished, ask your partner this question. They should spend about 20 seconds on their answer.

> • Which of these things would you prefer to do with your friends?

1 READING

1 You are going to read an extract from a novel about three girls. Look at the picture and answer these questions with a partner.

1 Where are the girls?
2 Do you think they know each other well?
3 One of them has some news. Do you think it's good news or bad news?

2 Read the text very quickly and answer these questions.

1 What news does Sierra give Amy and Vicki? How does she feel about it?
2 How does Amy feel about Sierra's news?
3 What do they make plans for?

Exam tip

Before you answer the questions, always read the text quickly to get an idea of what it is about. ✓

Exam task

In Reading Part 1, there are always eight multiple-choice questions about one text. The text below is shorter than in the exam and there are only four questions.

For questions 1–4 on page 11, choose the answer (A, B, C or D) which you think fits best according to the text.

Vicki swept past the tables to the counter. Watching her, Sierra thought about the contrast between her two friends. If Amy zigzagged through life with her head down, Vicki moved through her days at full speed, with her chin to the sky and the wind in her long, silky, brown hair. That zestful optimism eventually had linked Sierra and Vicki, even though Sierra originally had interpreted Vicki's bold approach to life as arrogance.

The instant Vicki returned to their table, Sierra spilled her news. "Okay, are you both ready for my big announcement?"

"It can't be that huge if you didn't tell me at lunch today and made me wait until now," Vicki said, carefully pouring her tea over the glass of crushed ice.

"I wanted to tell you both at the same time."

"I appreciate that," Amy said.

"So?" Vicki prompted.

"Last night my brother called and told me he's going to Southern California next week. He's pretty sure he wants to attend Rancho Corona University for his master's degree, but he wanted to check out some colleges before he made a final decision."

"That's your big news?" Vicki asked. Her pretty face took on a teasing grin. "You definitely could have told me that at lunch."

line 18

"Wait," Sierra said, her enthusiasm unruffled. "He's going to drive down there next week, and he asked if I wanted to go with him, and my parents said yes!"

"Good for you," Vicki said. "Bring back something for each of us."

"Didn't you go to California last year for Easter vacation?" Amy asked.

"Yes."

"And you also flew down there for your friends' wedding last summer." Amy turned her lower lip into a friendly pout. "How do you expect us to be happy for you again? You keep going on these adventures, and we don't go anywhere. I've never been to California – ever – in my life. I've only been to Seattle – once."

"I hope you have a good time," Vicki said cheerfully to Sierra.

Sierra broke into a wide grin. "You mean you hope we have a good time."

"'We' meaning you and Wes?" Vicki ventured. "Or 'we' meaning the three of us?"

"All of us!" Sierra spouted. "My brother is driving my parents' van down, and they said I could invite my friends to go."

"When do we leave?" Vicki asked.

"Wednesday after school," Sierra said.

The three friends bent their heads close. They began to make a plan for their upcoming road trip as the spring sunshine lit their little corner of the world. Sierra felt a gleeful rush of anticipation and knew it couldn't come fast enough for her.

Before you decide on your answer to each question, read the
tip above it to help you.

Underline the words in the text which give you the
answer to question 1.

1 What do we find out about Sierra's attitude
   towards her friends in the first paragraph?
   A She wishes Vicki and Amy were
      more similar to each other.
   B She feels more positively towards Vicki than
      she once did.
   C She always knew she and Vicki would be
      friends.
   D She thinks Amy has a better approach to life
      than Vicki.

Some questions ask you about a particular word or an
expression. Find the answer by reading the part of the
text before and after it very carefully. Find the answer
to question 2.

2 The writer uses the expression 'her enthusiasm
   unruffled' in line 18 to show that Sierra
   A wasn't put off by the reaction she received.
   B felt annoyed that she was being hurried.
   C felt confused about how she should continue.
   D didn't understand why she had to explain.

Find the part of the text where Amy is speaking and
answer question 3.

3 How does Amy react to Sierra's news?
   A She thinks Sierra isn't grateful enough for the
      opportunities she has.
   B She doesn't understand why Sierra wants to
      go away so much.
   C She thinks it's strange that Sierra keeps going
      to the same places.
   D She feels jealous of the experiences which
      Sierra is able to have.

Some questions ask you what a word like *it* or *that*
refers to. The answer may be in a different sentence or
in the same sentence. Underline *plan*, *road trip*, *spring
sunshine* and *rush of anticipation* in the last paragraph.
Read the whole paragraph and decide which can
replace *it* in the last sentence.

4 What couldn't come fast enough?
   A the plan
   B the road trip
   C the spring sunshine
   D the rush of anticipation

Vocabulary – Matching expressions with similar meanings

3 Expressions 1–7 below often appear in multiple-choice
   questions. Read the paragraph and think about what is
   happening. Underline the words which match the expressions
   below. Write the number of the phrase next to the part of the
   text it matches.

Marcus stood and watched as Jake came through the school gate. He realised
he couldn't trust Jake and now he wondered why he had always been so keen
to get his approval. Jake was walking in a way that Marcus had never noticed
before. He really thought he was better than the rest of them. He was headed
now towards a couple of boys who were standing near Marcus. Marcus saw
them look up. He realised Jake was asking one of them to do something. The
boy looked very unsure and worried – it must have been something that wasn't
allowed. The other boy relaxed, glad that it wasn't him who had been chosen.
Marcus started to feel rather annoyed about the way Jake behaved. Why should he make that boy
do something he didn't want to? Marcus suddenly made up his mind he would tackle Jake. He wasn't
going to let him get away with it this time.

1 eager to please   2 was arrogant   3 doubtful about something
4 seemed relieved   5 irritated   6 decided   7 stand up to

1 WRITING

Part 1: Email

1   Read the Part 1 task below and answer these questions.

  1   Who is Mrs Jones?
  2   What is she planning?
  3   Why does she use *could*?
  4   Look at the notes on the right. How many different points are there to reply to?

2   With a partner, discuss what you could say for each of the points.

> You have received this email from Mrs Jones, your English teacher. Read the email and the notes you have made. Then write an email of 120–150 words to Mrs Jones, using **all** your notes.

> From: Mrs Jones
>
> Sent: 10 June
>
> Subject: end-of-term picnic
>
> As it's nearly the end of term, I thought it would be good to organise a picnic so our class can celebrate together. ——— *Great!*
>
> Why don't we all bring some food and drink and share it? You could cook something or buy something at the shop. I'm going to bake some small cakes. What would you like to bring? ——— *Explain*
>
> We could have the picnic in the small park just opposite the school, or walk down to the river and picnic on the bank. Which do you think would be better? ——— *Tell Mrs Jones*
>
> Shall we just sit and chat, or do you have some other ideas about what we could do? ——— *Suggest ...*
>
> Reply soon
> Mrs Jones

3   Work in pairs. Now read the response below and answer these questions.

  1   Has Joanna responded to all the points Mrs Jones made?
  2   Has she written enough words?

> Dear Mrs Jones
>
> Thanks very much for your email. What an absolutely fantastic idea to have a picnic for our class at the end of term! We've been together for a whole year, so I think it will be nice to celebrate that.
>
> I'm afraid I'm not very good at cooking, but I'm sure I can make some sandwiches for everyone. I'll make some different kinds, so everyone can have something they like. And I'll buy a big bottle of orange at the local shop.
>
> In my view, it would definitely be better to have the picnic by the river. The weather is sunny and we can go swimming in the river if the water is warm enough. There's a big climbing area with trees and ropes we can go to as well.
>
> As for other ideas, why don't we ask Alex and Sammy to bring their guitars and ask them to play some songs for us?
>
> Best wishes
> Joanna

4   Work in pairs. Read Joanna's answer again and underline the phrases she uses to introduce:

A a positive comment   B an apology
C an opinion   D a suggestion

5   Here are some more phrases. Label them A, B, C or D.

  1   I'm sorry to say that   ....
  2   We could always   ....
  3   I'm so glad to hear that   ....
  4   For me, ...
  5   I was pleased to hear your news about   ....
  6   I'd recommend   ....
  7   How / What about ...*ing* something   ....
  8   I think / believe / feel that   ....

6   Work in pairs. Write an answer to Mrs Jones, using the phrases above. You should write 120–150 words.

7 Work in pairs. Read the email in the Exam task and answer these questions.

1 Who is Alex? How old do you think he is?
2 Will your reply be more or less formal than your reply to Mrs Jones? Why?

8 Look at the prompts on the right of the email. Are these statements true or false?

Point 1 You can refuse the invitation to the pool in your reply.
Point 2 You can say yes or no to going on the waterslides with Alex.
Point 3 You can choose either of the restaurants.
Point 4 You can say that being picked up at 7.00 a.m. is not OK.

9 Here are some phrases you might be able to use in your answer. Put a cross against any phrases which you should **not** use.

1 a Thanks very much. I would absolutely love to come to the pool with you!
  b It sounds great, but unfortunately I won't be able to come to the pool.
  c That's awesome, of course I'll come to the pool with you.

2 a As for the waterslides, I'm scared of heights, so I'd prefer not to go on them.
  b Waterslides – brilliant! I adore going down them and we'll have a great time.
  c I've never been down a waterslide, but why not, I'll give it a go!

3 a I'd rather go to the burger place, I don't like pizzas so much.
  b About the restaurant, I like both pizzas and burgers, so why don't you choose?
  c I really like Chinese food so shall we go to a Chinese restaurant?

4 a Thanks, don't bother though, I'll meet you there.
  b Thanks very much, I'd like to go with you because we can chat on the way.
  c Thanks for offering me a lift, it'll be much better than going on the bus!

10 Now do the Exam task. Ask your partner to check your work before you hand it in. Remember to expand some of the points!

Exam task

You have received this email from your English friend, Alex. Read Alex's email and the notes on it. Then write an email to Alex using all your notes.

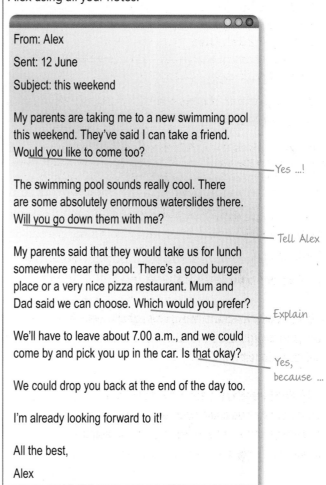

From: Alex

Sent: 12 June

Subject: this weekend

My parents are taking me to a new swimming pool this weekend. They've said I can take a friend. Would you like to come too?

— Yes ...!

The swimming pool sounds really cool. There are some absolutely enormous waterslides there. Will you go down them with me?

— Tell Alex

My parents said that they would take us for lunch somewhere near the pool. There's a good burger place or a very nice pizza restaurant. Mum and Dad said we can choose. Which would you prefer?

Explain

We'll have to leave about 7.00 a.m., and we could come by and pick you up in the car. Is that okay?

Yes, because ...

We could drop you back at the end of the day too.

I'm already looking forward to it!

All the best,

Alex

Write your email.

 See page 86

2 Exploring the world
READING — Adventure and travel

Part 2

1 Look at the young people in the photos. Work in pairs to answer the questions.

1 What are the teenagers doing? Have you ever done any of these things?
2 Do you think teenagers enjoy doing dangerous activities more than older people?

2 You are going to read about a boy called Parker who went to the North Pole. Look at the text. What does the title tell you?

3 Quickly read the text to understand what happened and answer the questions. Don't worry about the missing sentences.

a How far was the journey?   c What was the weather like?
b Who went with Parker?   d What problem did they have?

He nearly reached the top of the world

Few people have succeeded in skiing to the North Pole. (1) .... To do so, Parker had to cover 180 kilometres across snow and ice to reach his destination. (2) .... They had been accompanied by their parents but Parker was with just a guide called Doug. (3) .... During the journey they knew they would be faced with freezing wind and low temperatures. (4) .... Doug had experience of other problems too, like cracks appearing in the ice. (5) .... In fact, the gaps in the ice were much larger than they had expected because of global warming. (6) .... The gaps were just too wide for the two explorers to cross. So they had to give up and Parker travelled the last 15 miles in a helicopter, having been defeated by his reason for the trip – global warming.

4 Complete gaps 1–6 with sentences A–F.

A Two other teenagers had previously got there on skis but they had had a different starting point so had only gone half this distance.
B Teenager Parker Liautaud recently attempted to become one of them in order to draw attention to the effects of global warming.
C They have been known to reach –50°C in this part of the world.
D Parker had complete confidence in him because this would be his seventh trip.
E Doug hadn't seen anything as bad as that on his previous trips.
F These can appear faster than a man can walk and can become a real challenge.

5 Underline these words in the sentences in Exercise 4 and say what each one refers to in the story.

1 *there* (A) ....   3 *they* (C) ....   5 *that* (E) ....
2 *them* (B) ....   4 *him* and *his* (D) ....   6 *these* (F) ....

In Reading Part 2, there are seven paragraphs and eight sentences. The text below has four gaps and five sentences.

You are going to read a text written by a teenager about explorers. Four sentences have been removed from the text. Choose from the sentences A–E the one which fits each gap (1–4). There is one extra sentence which you do not need to use.

My future as an explorer

I've always wanted to be an explorer. When I was very small my favourite book was about adventurers and explorers and that's the one I always asked to have read to me. **1** [ ] I wanted to go to wild places, I knew I would do things no one else had done, like abseil down the highest mountain, or walk to the North Pole with only a polar bear for company.

I used to lie in bed and imagine that I was sleeping in a cabin in the middle of the Amazon Jungle with bears prowling outside, or in a tent in the Sahara Desert with tigers nearby. **2** [ ] There aren't any bears in the Amazon, or tigers in the Sahara.

I also used to think about the first sea explorers, sailing from their homes to the outer edge of the Earth, where they thought they might fall off the edge of the Earth, or be swallowed up by a sea monster. **3** [ ] They needed courage and trust to go out into the world. I knew that I wanted to be like that – I'd never be able to just sit around and accept the world as it is.

So I'm always pushing the limits. I always climb the tallest tree rather than the easiest, jump off the cliff into the sea rather than walk down, hold my breath underwater for longer than anyone else, try to cycle down the steepest hill near our house as fast as I can. **4** [ ] So I didn't try that again.

A Of course, at some point I realised that I'd got some of those details confused.

B They knew they could be killed at any moment through their lack of knowledge or poor judgement.

C I was aware that they were not the only ones who had done that.

D That last attempt ended in disaster, for the only thing I achieved was broken bones.

E Most of it went over my head, but the main theme stayed with me.

6 Work in pairs. Which words helped you choose? Which sentence doesn't fit and why?

Grammar – Past tenses

7 Read this text about Parker Liautaud and put the verb in brackets into the correct tense (past simple or past perfect).

Parker Liautaud **(1)** .... (attempt) to reach the North Pole. Two other teenagers **(2)** .... (reach) the North Pole previously. They **(3)** .... (travel) with their parents but Parker **(4)** .... (go) with a guide called Doug, who **(5)** .... (be) to the North Pole seven times before. Unfortunately, the cracks in the ice **(6)** .... (be) too large for them to cross. Doug **(7)** .... (not see) problems like that before on his other trips. In the end, they **(8)** .... (fly) the last part of the journey in a helicopter.

G *See page 79*

15

2 USE OF ENGLISH

Part 2

Grammar – Tenses and prepositions

1 ☉ Choose the correct word or words in italics in these sentences.

1 Yesterday I went shopping and I *'ve bought / bought* two fantastic T-shirts.
2 The shops were closed and we had to wait *to / until* the next day.
3 There were strange noises outside so I *looked / was looking* out of the window to see what *happened / was happening*.
4 There's nothing to do here *for / during* the winter.
5 I *'ve been trying / tried* to do this homework since I got home and I still *haven't finished / didn't finish*.
6 Last week as I *was coming / came* home, I *was seeing / saw* a strange animal.
7 There was a long queue because everybody had arrived *at / during* the same time.
8 Suddenly, my father realised he *'d forgotten / forgot* to lock the car.
9 I practised the piano every day *during / for* three weeks.
10 I looked everywhere for my purse but it *had disappeared / disappeared*.

2 Read the text below quickly to find out what it is about. Think about what kind of word is needed for each gap. Most of the missing words are prepositions or parts of verbs.

Exam task

In Use of English Part 2 there are 12 gaps. The text below has eight gaps and an example.

For questions 1–8, think of the word which best fits each gap. Use only one word in each gap. There is an example at the beginning (0). Use the grammar exercise above to help you.

Exam tip

You only ever need to write one word in the gap. It will never be a contraction like *didn't* as this is really two words (*did not*). ✓

THE MYSTERY OF THE BERMUDA TRIANGLE

The Bermuda Triangle is an imaginary triangle in the Atlantic Ocean. (0) ..For.. many years, people have told stories about mysterious disappearances that have (1) .... place in this area.

The explorer Christopher Columbus first wrote about the Bermuda Triangle in 1492. He (2) .... sailing across the Atlantic Ocean when he came (3) .... some mysterious light patterns in the sky. (4) .... the same time, his equipment started doing bizarre things.

It wasn't (5) .... the 1950s that the media became interested and several people published articles highlighting the disappearance of several ships and planes. They (6) .... all flown or sailed in the area and (7) .... of them was ever seen again. How did this happen? You can blame it on bad weather patterns, hurricanes or strange magnetic forces. Some people (8) .... even suggested aliens. Whatever the case, it's one of the great mysteries of our time.

The 'Mary Celeste', whose crew disappeared completely in the Atlantic Ocean in 1892.

Vocabulary – Word building (1)

3 Make adjectives from these nouns and verbs with the endings in the table.
Write them under the best heading.

accident adventure bear centre consider controversy culture desire fashion forget fury logic mystery nature predict rely remark suit universe

-able	-al	-ous

4 When you check your answers, look carefully at how the spelling changes if the
word ends in -y or -e. Write down some examples.

-y: ....

-e: ....

Exam task

In Use of English Part 3 there are ten gaps and words to change. The task below has eight gaps
and an example.

Use the word given in capitals at the end of some of the lines to form a word that
fits in the gap in the same line. There is an example at the beginning (0).

Exam tip

Each gap has its own word at
the end of the line that you must
change. Don't try to put that
word in any other gap. ✓

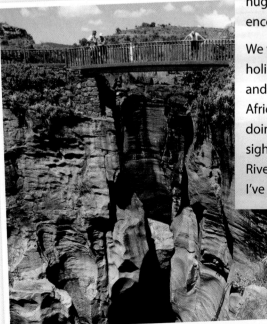

A TRIP TO REMEMBER

I've just been on an absolutely (0) ..unforgettable.. holiday   FORGET
with my family. My Dad decided that as my sister and I
are teenagers now, we could go on a really (1) ....   ADVENTURE
holiday. So he found a travel brochure which contained a
huge range of (2) .... trips including treks, wildlife   SUIT
encounters and (3) .... holidays.   CULTURE

We were spoilt for (4) ...., because there were   CHOOSE
holidays in all sorts of exciting (5) ...., like Peru, India   LOCATE
and China. However, in the end we decided to go to South
Africa because my sister's a keen (6) .... and she was   PHOTOGRAPH
doing a project on the (7) .... world. So we saw the   NATURE
sights in Cape Town and then went off to explore Blyde
River Canyon. It was one of the most (8) .... places   REMARK
I've ever seen.

2 SPEAKING | Where you live

Part 3

1 Think about a city or town you know or have visited. Tick (✔) the places you go/went to.

bowling alley ☐ cafés ☐ cinemas ☐ market ☐
museum ☐ shopping malls ☐ sports centre ☐
theatre ☐

Write them in order of importance for you. (most important = 1)

2 Compare your lists in a group. Use some of these expressions.

I think … is the most/least important because …
For me, … is less important than … because …
I'd prefer to go to / I'd rather go to … than … because …
My favourite place is ….
I would like to … but we don't have one.

3 Are there enough things for teenagers to do in your area? Which things would you like to be able to do?

4 Work in pairs. What are the people in the photos doing? Do teenagers enjoy going to these places in your country? Why?

5 You're going to work in a group of three. Think about how you will agree and disagree with the others. Mark these expressions A (agree) or D (disagree).

I don't think that's a good idea. …..   I agree with you. …..
I think it would be better to … …..   That's what I think too. …..
I think you're right. …..   I disagree. …..

Exam task

Work in groups of three. Your town wants to build new leisure facilities for young people. Discuss if the places in the photographs would be popular and decide which place should be built.

Part 4

6 Do you live in a city, town or village? Tick (✔) the words and expressions below you can use to talk about it.

mining ☐ fishing ☐ quiet ☐
mountain ☐ rural ☐ farming ☐
medium-sized ☐ university ☐
crowded ☐ sleepy ☐ capital ☐
historic ☐ modern ☐ wide streets ☐
a lot of traffic ☐ an old market square ☐
in the mountains ☐ not far from … ☐
in the middle of nowhere ☐ by a lake ☐
in the countryside ☐ in the centre of … ☐
in an area called … ☐

7 Now work with a partner. Use the words and expressions from Exercise 6 to answer these questions.

1 How would you describe your city/town/village?

> I live in an industrial city.

> My village is quite isolated.

2 What do you like about the place where you live? What do you dislike about it?

> I love living on the coast.

Exam task

Practise asking your partner his/her opinion on these questions.

- What are the advantages of living in the middle of a city? Why?
- Do you think it's better to live in a city, or in a village in the countryside? Why?
- Is it better for children to grow up in one place or move around? Why?

2 LISTENING

Part 1

1 Work in pairs. Look at the photos. How are the three cities different?

2 🔘 **1.05** Listen to a teenager talking about the city where she lives. Which city above is she talking about?

Now listen to the recording again. Write down all the words which helped you get the answer and compare with your partner.

3 🔘 **1.06** Read the following example of a Part 1 question. Listen to the recording and answer it.

You hear a girl talking about the city she lives in.
What does she particularly like about it?
A the shopping opportunities
B the different restaurants
C the outdoor festivals

4 🔘 **1.06** Listen again and read the script your teacher gives you. Underline the words which give you the answer. Why are the other answers wrong?

Exam task

In Listening Part 1 you will hear eight recordings and you will answer one question about each. There are four recordings in the task below.

🔘 **1.07** You will hear people talking in four different situations. For questions 1–4, choose the best answer (A, B or C).

1 You hear a boy talking to his aunt about his new school.
What is his opinion of the school?
A The behaviour of students is normally good.
B The design of the building encourages students to study.
C The teachers are better than those at his last school.

2 You will hear two people talking about a film they have just seen.
Which aspect of the film did they both like?
A the humour
B the setting
C the action

3 You will hear a girl talking about a school trip she has been on.
What did she learn about on the trip?
A the design of certain textiles
B the life of a designer
C the history of factory design

4 You will hear two teenagers talking about a friend.
What do they admire about him?
A He scores lots of goals.
B He encourages other players.
C He is cheerful despite an injury.

2 WRITING

Part 2: Story

1 Work in pairs. Read this first sentence of a story and the three short paragraphs below. Do they all follow from the first sentence?

Max heard someone calling his name excitedly, and turned to see who it was.

A It was his friend Peter, who rushed over saying that he'd won a prize, a trip to America. 'And there are four tickets,' he said. 'Do you want to come with us?'

B It was time to go so I jumped straight onto my bike and cycled into the forest along a dark and winding path.

C Anna came running down the path, laughing and crying at the same time. 'My Dad's got a new job in Australia, and it sounds great, but I'll have to leave all my friends behind.'

2 How could the story continue? Decide on some suitable endings with your partner.

Grammar – Past tenses

3 Work in pairs. Look at the pictures below and put them in the correct order to tell a story.

4 Discuss what happened in the story. Use these words and phrases.

> archaeologist   dig   fall into a hole   gold   Inca city   jungle   treasure

5 Stories are usually written in the past tense. Choose the correct form of the past tense verbs in the story.

It was very dark and I could hear strange noises all around me. I was in the jungle, (1) *looking / looked* for treasure. Everyone (2) *knew / was knowing* it was there, but no one (3) *had / has* ever found it. The local people told stories of a city full of gold which the Incas (4) *built / had built* centuries ago. Suddenly an owl (5) *hooted / has hooted*, and I (6) *was realising / realised* to my surprise that I could hear someone digging. 'Tim, is that you?' I (7) *was calling / called*. Tim (8) *was / had been* the other archaeologist working in the jungle. 'Yeah, come over here, I (9) *'ve / 'd* found a plate or something.' I (10) *was rushing / rushed* over to find Tim, without looking where I (11) *went / was going* and without warning I (12) *'ve disappeared / disappeared* down into a deep hole. Fortunately, I (13) *didn't / hadn't* hurt myself, and I could see something shining in the moonlight. Gold! Piles and piles of gold plates, vases, jewellery, swords! I (14) *'ve / 'd* found it – the gold everyone (15) *had / has* been looking for!

6 Divide the story above into three paragraphs, one for each section of the story.

Vocabulary – Adverbs and adjectives

7 Match the adjective with the correct noun in these sentences.

> courageous   intriguing   strong   worrying

1 When I walked into the room, I had a(n) .... sense that something was wrong.
2 Paula made a(n) .... attempt to win the marathon, but was beaten by her rival.
3 It's a(n) .... question, and I really want to know the answer to it.
4 Andrew suddenly had a(n) .... thought – what if the test was today?

> aggressive   brilliant   detailed   successful

5 Joanna made a(n) .... attempt on the school javelin record.
6 Max's .... attitude got him into a lot of trouble during his school years.
7 The deputy head drew up a(n) .... plan outlining every aspect of English teaching for the year.
8 It was a(n) .... solution to the problem, so we decided to put it into effect immediately.

8 Choose the correct adverb to go with the verb in these sentences.

1 The headmaster spoke *bitterly / calmly* to the little boy and he soon settled down.
2 The audience reacted very *positively / optimistically* to the second contestant in the talent competition.
3 Our teacher acted *carelessly / decisively* when she heard the fire bell and got everybody out of the school building immediately.
4 Patrick moved forward *clumsily / rapidly* and scored the goal that won the match.
5 All the parents agreed that the prize-giving ceremony was run very *efficiently / poorly*.
6 Lucy sat in the dentist's surgery waiting *patiently / hopefully* for her appointment.
7 The science teacher told his pupils to watch *hopefully / closely* as he carried out the experiment.
8 My best friend made an effort to visit me *rarely / regularly* when I was in hospital for a while.

> **Exam tip**
>
> Your story will read better and get a better mark if you can use some interesting and varied vocabulary and use words that go together well. These are known as collocations.

Grammar – Adverb formation

9 Make adjectives from these adverbs.

1 bitterly ....
2 clumsily ....
3 happily ....
4 hopefully ....
5 miserably ....
6 positively ....
7 politely ....
8 rapidly ....
9 rarely ....
10 simply ....

Now use the adverbs and adjectives above to answer these questions.

1 Which adjectives change their last letter to *-i* before adding *-ly*?
2 What happens to adjectives ending in a consonant and *-le*?
3 What happens to other adjectives ending in *-e*?
4 What happens to adjectives ending in *-l*?

G *See page 79*

Exam task

You have been asked to write a story for your school magazine. Your story must begin with this sentence:
I was amazed when I saw who was sitting in the seat opposite mine on the train.

Write your story.

Remember to:
- decide on your storyline before you start writing.
- make sure your story follows from the prompt sentence.
- use past tenses and write in paragraphs.
- try to use a range of interesting adjectives, adverbs and collocations.
- write 120–180 words.

W *See page 88*

3 The entertainment industry
LISTENING Films

 A
 B
 C
 D

Part 4

1 Work in pairs. Complete the table with the words and phrases connected with making a film.

acts   arranges the scenery   checks quality of voice recording
designs/fits costumes   does action shots
does someone's face/hair   films a scene   performs
plays a part/role   raises money to make the film
takes a shot of something   tells the actors what to do

Person	What (s)he does
actor	acts,
stuntman/woman	
set decorator	
director	
cameraman/woman	
producer	
costume designer	
sound technician	
make-up artist	

2 The people in the pictures work in the film industry. Use the words above to describe them and say what they are doing.

3 Look at the Exam task opposite and the underlining in question 1. Underline two or three important words in the instructions and in each question.

4 What do the instructions and questions tell you about what you will hear? Tick (✔) the topics you think Tania will talk about.

how she became famous ☐
her reactions to her own acting ☐
her own personality ☐
her favourite film ☐
a problem she has had ☐
her opinion of the director ☐
her daily routine ☐

Exam task

In Listening Part 4 there are seven multiple-choice questions. In the task below there are four.

🔘 **1.08** You will hear part of an interview with a young actor called Tania West. For questions 1–4, choose the best answer A, B or C.

1 Tania <u>describes seeing herself</u> on screen as
   A rather <u>frightening</u>.
   B slightly <u>unreal</u>.
   C a bit <u>boring</u>.

2 In what way is Tania like Angie, the character she plays in the film?
   A She doesn't get on well with other people.
   B She doesn't try to impress people.
   C She doesn't always behave as other people expect.

3 What did Tania find difficult about being on set?
   A working with older actors
   B learning her lines
   C having little time to relax

4 What does Tania say about her acting schedule?
   A She often filmed at night.
   B She had little trouble getting up early.
   C She missed having regular meals.

Exam tip

Underlining important words helps you to listen for the answer and predict what you will hear. ✔

3 WRITING

Part 2: Review

1 Work in pairs. Answer the questions below.

1 What is your favourite type of film? Tick (✔) the one(s) you like best.

action films ☐ animations ☐ cartoons ☐ comedies ☐ documentaries ☐
horror films ☐ romantic comedies (romcoms) ☐ science fiction films ☐
thrillers ☐ westerns ☐

2 What makes a film enjoyable? Tick (✔) the things you think are most important.

the acting ☐ the casting ☐ the direction ☐ the location ☐ the music ☐
the plot ☐ the script ☐ the special effects ☐ the stunts ☐

2 Look at the photos and discuss the questions in your pairs.

1 Do you recognise the heroes? Who are they? Who is your favourite hero?
2 Do you have any special heroes, real or imaginary, in your country? Describe them.

3 Read the Exam task below and answer the questions.

1 Can you write about a comedy, thriller or horror film? Yes or no? Why?
2 Can you write a negative opinion of the film? Yes or no? Why?

> Your English teacher has asked you to write a review for the school magazine of a film which has an impressive hero. Describe the film and the hero. Say what happens in the film and explain whether you would recommend it to other people.

4 Read the exam candidate's review and answer the questions.

1 Does the review give a clear impression of the film and the characters in it?
2 Does it make you want to see the film? Why? / Why not?
3 What tense is used in the review? Could you use any other tense?
4 Why does the review have a title? Which sentence sums up the candidate's opinion?

Batman: The Dark Knight

This is a dark, difficult and at times rather disturbing film, which really makes you think. As you sit in the audience, you wonder what would happen if a hero like Batman really came along and decided to deal with organised crime in our big cities, yet you are also entertained because the film has a lot of amazing action scenes.

In *The Dark Knight*, Batman is an action hero, but more importantly he is also a symbol of justice. He is a brave and determined character who teams up with the forces of law and order in the city of Gotham, ready to take on all the crime lords. As a result, he has to face a psychopathic and very scary villain called The Joker.

In my opinion, this film is outstanding. It is not only thrilling but it also makes you feel as if you are experiencing what is going on. When I saw it, everyone in the audience was totally involved in it, so I'd say it's a film you really must see.

5 Underline the adjectives and phrases the candidate uses to describe the film, Batman and the Joker. Write them under the correct heading. Is each one positive (P) or negative (N)?

Film   Batman   Joker

dark (N)

6 You should always write a brief plan before you start writing. Complete this plan for the review of *Batman: The Dark Knight*.

> *Batman: The Dark Knight*
>
> Para 1 introduction – describe the film, makes you .... + amazing .... scenes
>
> Para 2 content of film – describe Batman and his .... and how he fights organised .... and The ....
>
> Para 3 conclusion – sum up film and .... it (explain why)

7 Underline any linking words/phrases in the review which you could use yourself.

It is not only thrilling, but it also makes you ...

8 Look back at the types of film you ticked in Exercise 1 (page 23). Which film would you write about if you had to write a review of one of them? Tell your partner.

Exam task

Choose one of the exam tasks below. Decide which film you are going to write about and write your plan (three paragraphs) before writing your review, in 120–180 words.

1 You have seen this English-language advertisement on a teenage website.

> ### Film reviews wanted! The best thriller ever
>
> Have you seen a really exciting thriller recently? Write a review telling us about it. You should include information about the plot, the action scenes and the characters, and tell us whether you would recommend the film.
>
> **The best film reviews will be posted on our website next month.**

Write your **review**.

2 You have seen this announcement in an international magazine for young people.

> ### Film reviews wanted! Romantic comedies
>
> Have you seen a really enjoyable romantic comedy recently? Write a review telling us about the characters and what happens in the film, and say whether you would recommend the film to your friends.
>
> **The best reviews will be published in our magazine next month.**

Write your **review**.
- Make sure you give the name of the film.
- Plan your writing; write at least three paragraphs.
- Try to use some colourful vocabulary from the unit.
- Use some of the linking words/phrases from the unit.
- Write 120–180 words.

 See page 89

3 READING Music

Part 3

1 Answer the questions below and then compare your answers with a partner.

1 What sort of music do you like best? Why?

| pop heavy metal rock 'n' roll classical jazz rap hip hop salsa punk soul music |

2 Look at the picture. Which instruments would a rock band, a jazz band and a classical orchestra use?

2 Read the statements and the album review below. Tick (✔) the statements which match information in the review. Put a cross against the statements which say something different.

The album

contains songs whose words will appeal to a certain age group.	1	
contains songs which will tend to have a negative effect on people's emotions.	2	
will probably be less well received than the band's last one.	3	
takes a completely different approach from the band's last one.	4	
is likely to extend the success of the band.	5	
has a singer whose particular style has been well matched to the songs he sings.	6	
has a singer who should be given more chances to sing.	7	

'Probable and possible' by Miracle

All the songs on this album have lyrics which focus on the kinds of emotions that teenagers will really relate to but there's no way you could describe it as depressing.

Last autumn, the band Miracle brought out a long-awaited album which upset a lot of fans because it introduced a whole new sound. However, that album brought in new fans like me. *Probable and possible* develops that sound and is expected to further widen the band's appeal so it seems things can only go up for them from here.

Bradley, one of the singers, has a very unusual voice and he needs the right song. He only sings on a couple of numbers but they suit him perfectly. The rest of the singing is done by Kez, whose voice is amazing. Overall, there is almost nothing to criticise here.

3 Quickly read through the texts on page 26 and answer these questions. Spend only three minutes reading the texts.

1 Are the reviews all positive?
2 Would you like to listen to any of these albums?
3 Do any of them sound like albums you already listen to?

In Reading Part 3 there are between four and six texts and you answer 15 questions. The texts below are shorter and there are only nine questions.

You are going to read some reviews of music albums. For questions 1–9, choose from the albums (A–D). The albums may be chosen more than once.

Which album

might be difficult to follow with one of the same quality?	1
contains songs which can sound quite similar to each other?	2
contains songs about subjects often avoided?	3
will continue to appeal to the same people in future years?	4
would be improved without the inclusion of certain songs?	5
has been looked forward to for some time?	6
has a song which stands out but not because everyone will recognise it?	7
has songs which are unusual in combining both excellent music and words?	8
contains a song which gets louder as it goes on?	9

Grammar – Linking words and phrases

4 ◉ Find an example in the texts of each linker underlined below. Then correct the mistakes in these sentences.

1 <u>While</u> the fact that we were given a lot of homework, I managed to finish it all.

2 I like cycling to school. <u>Although</u> I don't like cycling in heavy traffic.

3 I took my brother to see a western <u>despite</u> I don't like westerns myself.

4 <u>However</u> I enjoyed the concert, I wouldn't say it was the best I'd been to.

5 In the winter I play football. <u>In spite of</u> in the summer I play tennis too.

6 <u>Even though</u> playing the guitar very well, Anita has never learnt to read music.

G See page 80

THIS WEEK'S BEST ALBUM RELEASES

A *Pedal Street* by Breeze
Reviewer Anna Martino, age 13
Breeze has released *Pedal Street* after a two-year wait, in spite of pressure from fans and their record company to do so earlier. Fans had been told to expect something special and this is a masterpiece. With drummer Tom Wiseman's strong rhythms, and bassist Miguel Sandro's fantastic harmonies, this band's music is exceptional. The song lyrics express emotions that are felt by everybody, focusing on topics other artists seem to prefer not to sing about. Lead singer Josh Smith's voice is so emotional that it feels as though he's sitting right in front of you. Breeze use an interesting mix of styles including classical strings and modern guitar riffs.

B *Thrill* by Skydiggers
Reviewer Alexis Walker, age 14
Skydiggers, a Canadian rock group, have released the album *Thrill*, which was recorded over two years. Suzi Tarrant begins with high-pitched, smooth vocals, drawing you into the soft sound of her voice. However, she then shows just what the band is about with the roaring, angry growl that follows. Although some tunes are difficult to distinguish from each other in the sense that Tarrant's voice doesn't vary from song to song, the album will soon be permanently fixed on your playlist. On many albums, the best song is not the most well known and that is certainly the case here – the song 'Up to here' is in a class of its own.

C *Silver Honeybees* by Lena and the Lantanas
Reviewer Sam Roberts, age 16
Lena and her band, the Lantanas, tie together both contemporary and soul music in this album. Lena's been allowed to sing all types of songs here, including acoustic ballads and jazz-pop, in order to really show what she can do. And in case you think that her new far-ranging style may not appeal to a youthful teenage fan base, remember that her teen audience is sure to mature and grow along with her as she makes more music. While some bands incorporate good beats but have cliché lyrics that make you feel slightly sick, or sing songs with meaningful words yet make a dreadful sound, the Lantanas are by contrast a rare find.

D *Hungry Rock* by April Sapa
Reviewer Julie Zhang, age 14
April Sapa's debut album shows her liking for punk which she mixes with pop-rock. This first album will set high standards for her second, but it also shows that she has room to grow. Despite having a more limited vocal range than her sister, who is also a singer, April proves that she does have a big talent for writing. The album covers everything a teenager can feel: love, hate, acceptance, defiance and even boredom. It is an excellent combination of easy listening, even though there are several songs that could have easily been left out, resulting in a better album overall.

3 SPEAKING

What might people enjoy about these different types of films?

Why is music important to these different groups of people?

Part 1

1 Look at question 1 and the candidate's answer below. Then write your answers for questions 1–6, add extra information, and an additional comment and/or opinion.

Films and Cinema

1 Do you usually watch films on television, or at the cinema?
2 If you go to the cinema, when do you go, and who with?
3 What is your favourite type of film and why?

Music

4 Have you ever been to a concert? Did you enjoy it?
5 When and how do you like listening to music?
6 Do you play a musical instrument? Which one?

| extra information | answer |

I don't live near a cinema so I watch a lot of films on TV and DVD. It's a great way to relax in the evening and I like to watch with my family or friends.

| additional comment/opinion |

2 Now take it in turns to ask each other the questions.

Exam tip

Don't just give one-word answers. Try to give extra information. Then add a comment or opinion. ✓

Part 2

3 Work in pairs. Make a list of things you can say about the pictures above.

4 [1.09] Now listen to two candidates talking about the pictures. Did they have the same ideas as you? Tick (✔) the ideas that are on your list.

5 [1.09] Listen again. Both the candidates needed words they didn't know. Complete the phrases they used to explain what they meant.

1 ... you know, the .... films which have ...., not actors
2 ... these people are ... well, ... a bank has just been robbed or .... that.
3 It's a .... street dance I don't know the .... of ...
4 ... the children in the photo of the school orchestra look very ... well ... er ... um ... . relaxed.

6 The candidates avoided four words they didn't know. What were they?

7 [1.10] Listen to the last part of each conversation again and tick (✔) the phrases the candidates used to answer these questions.

Which of the films would you prefer to see?
Which of the activities would you prefer to do?
I'd rather ... than ... ☐   I'd prefer to ... ☐   I'd sooner ... ☐
I think it's better to ... ☐   I'd definitely ... ☐

Exam task

Now you are each going to talk about two of the pictures for one minute. Ask your partner the question above the pictures and time him/her for one minute.

Exam tip

If you don't know a word, use a phrase to explain it. ✓

3 USE OF ENGLISH

Part 4

Grammar – The passive

1 🔘 **1.09** Look at these sentences from Speaking Part 2. Complete them with the correct tense of the passive. Check your answers by listening again.

Candidate A

1 A mouse .... by a cat and I suppose .... soon.
2 ... a bank .... or something like that. That's why the men in the black car .... by the police. .... soon.

Candidate B

3 The music .... on a sound system with huge speakers.
4 I guess some of them .... to do it by their parents or teacher.
5 I expect the concert .... by the parents.

2 Now write the verbs in the correct column in the table. (You won't find an example of every tense.)

	verb form	past participle
present simple		
present continuous	is/are being	chased
future simple		
past simple		
present perfect		
past perfect		
with modals		

3 There are eight more examples of the passive in Reading Part 3 (look at the questions and the texts) on page 26. Underline them and add them to the table.

4 🔘 Now correct the mistakes in the passive in these sentences written by exam candidates.

1 This castle has been builded in the twelfth century.
2 I was give a leaflet which contained some interesting information.
3 The band first established in 1992.
4 These days music has been making by computers.
5 My best friend called Ann-Marie.
6 The concert supposed to start at 7.00, but the guitarist arrived late.
7 My house located in a beautiful area.
8 The business studies course cancelled at the last minute.
9 Will lunch include in the price of the school trip?
10 My family stay in a house that situated a few miles from the beach.

5 In Use of English Part 4 you have to complete a sentence using a prompt word, so that it means the same as the original above it. You can write only two to five words in the gap. Choose the correct answer for these examples. Why are the other answers wrong?

1 A number of reviewers on teenage websites have recommended Tom Cox's new book.

BEEN

Tom Cox's new book .... on teenage websites.

A has been strongly recommended
B had been strongly recommended
C is being strongly recommended

2 Everyone was disappointed when the headmaster cancelled the trip at the last moment.

WAS

To everyone's .... by the headmaster at the last moment.

A disappointed the trip was cancelled
B disappointment the trip was cancelled
C disappointment the trip had to be cancelled

3 We thought the school concert was going to end at 9.00, but it didn't finish until 10.00.

SUPPOSED

The school concert .... finished at 9.00 but it went on until 10.00.

A is supposed to be
B was supposed to
C was supposed to be

4 My older brother has got a job interview tomorrow.

BEING

My older brother .... a job tomorrow.

A is being interviewed for
B being interviewed for
C is being interviewed to

5 I'd prefer to watch the football on TV tonight.

RATHER

I .... the football on TV tonight.

A 'd rather to watch
B rather to watch
C 'd rather watch

G *See page 80*

Exam task

In Use of English Part 4 there are eight questions. There are five in the task below.

Complete the second sentence so that it has a similar meaning to the first sentence, using the word given. Do not change the word given. You must use between two and five words, including the word given.

Exam tip

Remember you can only use two to five words and that you usually have to make more than one change. If you have written more than five words (a word like *I've* counts as two words), you have made a mistake. ✓

1 The Romans constructed the fort overlooking the hill nearly 2000 years ago.

BUILT

The fort overlooking the hill .... the Romans nearly 2000 years ago.

2 A small boy on a skateboard knocked my sister over yesterday.

WAS

My sister .... a small boy on a skateboard yesterday.

3 The radio stations have played that music track over a hundred times this week.

HAS

That music track .... than a hundred times this week by the radio stations.

4 By this time next week we'll have given all our projects to our English teacher.

HANDED

By this time next week all our projects .... to our English teacher.

5 Anna Hamilton will wear one of Dior's dresses to the opening night.

BE

One of Dior's dresses .... Anna Hamilton to the opening night.

4 Active life

READING   Sports

Part 1

1   Look at the list of sports below. Which do you think are the five most popular sports in the world? Which sports are most popular in your country?

.... athletics	.... badminton	.... cricket
.... cycling	.... football	.... gymnastics
.... hockey	.... ice skating	.... martial arts
.... snowboarding	.... surfing	.... tennis
.... volleyball	.... windsurfing	.... yoga

2   We *do* athletics, we *play* badminton and we *go* cycling. Write the correct verb in Exercise 1. Add any other sports that you enjoy to the list.

3   Look at the sports in Exercise 1 and answer the questions.

    1   Have you ever done any of them?
    2   Do you enjoy watching any of them?
    3   Which sport(s) would you like to try?
    4   Who is your favourite sportsperson and why?

4   Which words in the box below can you use to talk about football / tennis? Three words don't match either sport. What kind of sport are they used for?

> court   defender   goalkeeper   lap   net
> opponent   penalty   pitch   point   race
> referee   serve   tackle   track   umpire

5   Read the text *Future football stars* quickly to get an idea of what it is about.

Which paragraph
A   makes a comparison between success in football and in other areas?
B   describes the advantages of being at a football academy?
C   suggests how some boys react when they are chosen for a football academy?
D   explains what a football academy is?

In Reading Part 1 there is a long text and there are eight questions based on it. The text below is shorter and there are four questions on it.

Exam tip

There are usually one or two questions about each paragraph. The questions are always in the same order as the text. ✓

You are going to read an extract from a newspaper article. For questions 1–4, choose the answer (A, B, C or D) which you think fits best according to the text.

FUTURE FOOTBALL STARS

Football academies were set up by leading football clubs like Manchester United and Liverpool so their coaches could run trials to identify and train talented boys from as young as eight as potential players for their first team. All the big football clubs have one, and other less well-known teams run their own schools of excellence.

This means that in Britain there are at least 9,000 boys at any one time attending academies after school who think they are going to be a famous footballer. Unfortunately, for most this isn't the case. One eight year old was selected for Chelsea academy and he went from being top of his class at school to being the boy who was messing around at the back. His mother asked him why he wasn't trying hard at school any more. His reply was that he was going to be a goalkeeper and be rich so he didn't need to. In the end, he only lasted a year in the academy but, luckily for him, he was still young enough to recover and not be so discouraged that he never played football again.

But football is not unique. Any sport or other field where only a few can get to the top has an invisible layer of also-rans. These people are very talented and do their absolute best but ultimately it will not pay off because they are just not exceptional enough. In football, this effect is magnified because the numbers of players selected for training by academies is so huge. Most of these won't get into a team and most won't become professionals.

This doesn't put off all the boys who are spotted by the big football clubs and are desperate to join the academies. The benefits are still there for them of course. They get to play as much football as possible – the coaches teach them to pass, tackle and practise standard techniques, moves and penalty kicks over and over again. The skills become part of them as they are with professional players, so they are automatic and the boys don't have to think about them when they're on the pitch. Experts say this is the way to do it, otherwise you end up with players who are much more likely to get injured.

Before you decide on your answer to each question, read the tip above it to help you.

Underline 'one' then read the text before and after that word. The words in the options are all in the text.

1 What does 'one' refer to in line 5?
   A a trial
   B a coach
   C a first team
   D an academy

Find the reference to the boy's mother. Read the whole paragraph before answering the question.

2 What did one boy's mother notice after he joined an academy?
   A His schoolwork suffered because football took up too much time.
   B There was little support at school for his changed circumstances.
   C There was a significant change in his attitude towards school.
   D He refused to play football at school any more.

Find 'an invisible layer of also-rans' and underline it. Don't worry if you don't understand it as it will be explained in the text. Underline the explanation and then answer the question.

3 What is the writer referring to by 'an invisible layer of also-rans' in the third paragraph?
   A those footballers who will not in the end be rewarded for their hard work
   B the fact that there are fewer opportunities for professional footballers than there used to be
   C the number of footballers who are not willing to put in the amount of effort required
   D the fact that the wrong people are sometimes selected to play in the best teams

There are several benefits mentioned in the text. Which one matches one of the options?

4 What advantage of the academies is mentioned in the fourth paragraph?
   A The coaches can adapt techniques to suit individual players.
   B The players are trained in a way which results in fewer injuries.
   C There are experts to answer the players' questions.
   D There are more opportunities to watch professional players in action.

4 LISTENING

Part 2

1 Read these sentences about a girl who rides mountain bikes. Which one needs an adjective in the gap?

FREYA STANLEY – DOWNHILL MOUNTAIN BIKER

Freya was given her first mountain bike by her [1].

Freya nearly lost her last race because of a [2].

The last thing Freya checks before a race is the [3].

Freya thinks the most important thing about clothes is that they are [4].

2 Which gap in Exercise 1 could each of these words go in?

brakes brother comfortable friend photographer post rock route sister stylish tight tree tyres uncle warm weather

3 🔊 **1.11** Listen to Freya. Choose the word she says for each gap.

Exam task

In Listening Part 2 you will hear a long recording and answer ten questions on it. The task below has six questions.

🔊 **1.12** You will hear an interview with a young skater called Karl Milton. For questions 1–6, complete the sentences.

KARL MILTON – SKATER

Karl came in [1] place in a competition last week.

Karl thinks about the [2] when he is performing in a competition.

The most important thing for skaters when practising is to remember to [3].

Going [4] in his spare time benefits Karl's skating skills.

Karl will appear in a TV programme called [5].

In the TV show competitors can choose their own [6].

Exam tip

You usually need to write one word but sometimes you will write two or three words. The word(s) you write should be exactly what you hear. ✓

Grammar – Modal verbs

4 Complete the gaps in what Karl said with one of the modal verbs given. Listen again if you need to.

can can't have to should

1 The skaters .... show that they are able to do all the main moves.
2 They .... choose who they skate with.
3 They .... follow a certain routine.
4 They .... decide which music they want to skate to.

could have won
must have been practising
should have been

5 I .... in the team four years ago ... but I was left out.
6 Janine Graham .... all the time as she was even better than last year.
7 Either of us .... but we weren't quite good enough.

5 Which sentence in Exercise 4 mentions something which:

is allowed .... seems certain ....
is advised .... isn't allowed ....
was possible .... is a rule ....
was expected ....

6 ⊙ Now choose the correct verb in these sentences.

1 My family goes for a walk on Sundays when we *mustn't / don't have to* work.
2 The show *must / should* have started at 7.30 but it started at 8.15.
3 I don't remember the date but it *should have been / must have been* a Friday.
4 You *mustn't / can't* miss the chance to see this amazing film.
5 He *must / had to* be quick because he didn't have much time to get there.
6 The first time Steve was late, his mother was worried that something *must / should* have happened to him.

G *See page 81*

4 SPEAKING

Part 3

> • What are the advantages of each activity for getting fit and having fun?

1 Look at the activities above, available at a sports centre. Make notes to answer the question above the photos. For each activity, think about:

- how fit you need to be
- if you can do the activity with other people
- how easy it is to learn
- if you would like to do it regularly
- how competitive it is

2 Work in pairs to discuss the question in Exercise 1. Ask your partner's opinion and react to what they say. Here are some useful expressions.

Asking your partner's opinion
What do you think?
What would you choose?
How about you?
Do you think it's best to ...?
Shall we start with ...?

Reacting to your partner
Do you think so?
Really?
It's not the same for me because ...
I feel the same because ...

3 Now change partners and do the Exam task below. Your discussion should last for about three minutes. Time yourselves.

Exam task

Your local sports centre has an open day and is offering free classes in two activities. You are going with your friends. You can choose martial arts, dancing, volleyball, basketball, gymnastics or badminton.

First, talk to each other about the advantages of choosing each activity. Then decide which two you would each choose.

Part 4

4 In Speaking Part 4 you are asked for your opinions on a topic connected to Speaking Part 3, for example:

Do you think people of your age do enough sport or do they prefer to watch TV?

Look at these opinions. Do you agree with any of them?

> It's much easier to watch TV or go on the computer than make an effort to do sport.

> It can be expensive to do sport because you have to pay for somewhere to play.

> Well, teenagers do watch a lot of TV but watching sport on TV encourages you to go and do it.

> I think the problem is that there aren't enough places to do sport.

5 Can you think of other answers to the question?

Exam tip
The examiner will ask you several questions so the discussion lasts for four minutes. Don't worry if you can't think of more to say as there will be another question. ✓

Exam task

Work in pairs to answer the questions.

- Should there be more opportunities to do different sports at school?
- Why are some sports less popular than others?
- How can people who don't like competitive sport be encouraged to get fit?

USE OF ENGLISH Keeping fit and healthy

Part 2

Grammar – Prepositions following verbs and adjectives

1 ⊘ Choose the correct preposition in these sentences.

1 What happens now depends *on / of* what our teacher decides.
2 Parents are responsible *of / for* what their children do.
3 Jose always had excellent marks so I was very jealous *of / about* him.
4 I would like to help *for / with* the concert tonight.
5 When children get bored they start complaining *about / for* everything.
6 The dance I did is typical *of / from* the south of Spain.
7 I've been thinking *about / of* your problem and what you should do.
8 I'm so excited *for / about* the party tomorrow.
9 I'm very interested *in / about* learning the guitar.
10 I talked *at / to* my friends about your idea and they want to come.

> **Exam tip**
>
> Learn verbs and adjectives with their prepositions as they are often tested in Use of English Part 2. ✓

Exam task

> **Exam tip**
>
> Read the text quickly first, then write the missing words in the gaps. When you have finished, read the whole text again. Check that the words you've written make sense. ✓

In Use of English Part 2 there are 12 gaps and an example. There are nine gaps and an example in the task below.

For questions 1–9, read the text below and think of the word which best fits each gap. Use only one word in each gap. There is an example at the beginning (0).

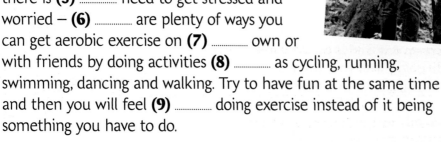

ENJOYABLE EXERCISE

You **(0)** .have. probably heard countless times how exercise will keep you fit and healthy. But getting **(1)** .... right amount can also increase your energy levels and even help improve your mood too. Experts recommend that teenagers get 60 minutes or more of physical activity **(2)** .... day. Many teenagers achieve this by getting involved **(3)** .... team sports such as football. But if you're not keen **(4)** .... playing team sports there is **(5)** .... need to get stressed and worried – **(6)** .... are plenty of ways you can get aerobic exercise on **(7)** .... own or with friends by doing activities **(8)** .... as cycling, running, swimming, dancing and walking. Try to have fun at the same time and then you will feel **(9)** .... doing exercise instead of it being something you have to do.

Part 3

Vocabulary – Word building (2)

2 Look at the words in the second column. Make a noun from each one and write the suffix in the last column.

		Noun	Noun suffix
Adjectives	SILENT	silence	̶T̶ + CE
	SIMILAR	....	....
Verbs	CONCLUDE	....	....
	SUGGEST	....	....

> **Exam tip**
> You may need to add some extra letters or change some letters before you add a suffix. ✓

3 Make nouns from these words, using the same suffixes.

Adjectives: confident convenient curious equal generous independent patient possible
Verbs: appreciate concentrate connect decorate divide expand produce react

Exam task

In Use of English Part 3, there is an example and ten words to change. The task below has an example and five words.

Use the word given in capitals at the end of the line to form a word that fits in the gap in the same line. There is an example at the beginning (0).

FAST FOOD GETS HEALTHY

Fast food is big business, with hamburgers and pizzas leading the way. But these two **(0)** European dishes did not get the fast food treatment until the world's first fast food restaurant opened in San Bernardino, California, in 1948. Restaurant owners wanted to take advantage of the rising **(1)** .... of cars, so they made a **(2)** .... to design drive-in restaurants. They simplified their menus so that there was no **(3)** .... for a knife, spoon or fork and they used cups, plates and bags that could be thrown away. By the 1960s and 1970s this kind of food was becoming **(4)** .... common in Europe and since then it has spread to other parts of the world. The most recent trend has been the **(5)** .... of more healthy options like salads to menus and this looks likely to continue.

EUROPE

POPULAR
DECIDE

NECESSARY
INCREASE
INTRODUCE

Vocabulary – Food

4 Make adjectives that you can use to describe food from these nouns.

fat nut salt spice taste

5 Which of the adjectives below can you use to describe these nouns?
(You can use some of the adjectives twice.)

.... diet .... meat .... fruit .... pudding

balanced fried healthy low-fat raw rich ripe rotten
seasonal sugary tough vegetarian

WRITING

Part 1: Letter

1 Work in pairs. Read the exam task below and answer these questions.

1 Who is Peter Cliff?
2 Why has he written a letter? What does he want to know?
3 Does he use formal or informal language? Underline some examples in the letter which show this.

Your English teacher has asked you to reply to this letter from Peter Cliff, a cyclist who is going to give a talk to your class. Read Peter Cliff's letter and the notes you have made. Then write a letter to Mr Cliff, using all your notes.

I will be pleased to come and give a talk to your class on the afternoon of 3rd March. —— Thank Mr Cliff

I always like to know something about the students I am talking to, so please could you tell me something about your class and your level of English? —— Explain

I could either talk about my training and how I keep fit, or I could talk about some of the races I have done recently. Which would you prefer? —— Tell Mr Cliff

I can spend two hours with your class, so is there anything else you would like me to do during that time? —— Ask Mr Cliff to ...

I look forward to meeting you

Yours sincerely

Peter Cliff

Exam tip

The difference between formal and informal written English is becoming less clear. But, before you reply, look carefully at how formal the language in the input email or letter is. Don't mix formal and informal language.

---

2 How will you begin and end the reply you write?

3 Now read this reply, which has some missing phrases. Choose the most formal/polite answer from the lists below to complete the reply. All of them are grammatically correct.

Dear Mr Cliff
(1) .... for agreeing to come and talk to our class.
We are fourteen years old, and our level of English is intermediate. We are all quite interested in sport, but we don't know much about cycling. (2) ...., because we are not used to English people speaking very fast.
(3) .... about training and keeping fit, as several people in the class are interested in this. However, if there is time, you could talk about some of the races you have done as well.
Finally, (4) .... us a film or slides of you in action on your bike.
We are looking forward to your talk.
Yours sincerely
Martin Fischer

---

1 A Thanks
  B Thank you very much
  C Thank you

2 A Please could you talk slowly
  B You must talk slowly
  C We would be grateful if you talked slowly

3 A Speak
  B I think it would be better if you spoke
  C Could you speak

4 A what about showing
  B you could show
  C I wonder if it would be possible for you to show

4 Read this letter from your English penfriend, Chris. Underline some examples which show the relationship between you and Chris. How is it different from your relationship with Mr Cliff? Is it more or less formal?

I'm so glad you're coming to stay with me next month! — Me too!

I usually do an activity at the local sports club during the first week of the holidays, and I'm planning to do volleyball this time. Would you like to do volleyball too? — No, because ...

If you don't want to do that, you can do tennis, football or swimming instead. Would you rather do one of those? — Yes, explain

And shall I send you some more info about those sports? — Yes, ask Chris to find out about ...

Write back soon.

Best wishes

Chris

5 Work in pairs. Decide which of the following (A, B or C) you could use for each prompt and why you can't use the other(s). Sometimes more than one answer is possible.

1 **A** Yes, I'm really pleased about my visit too!
   B Yes, it'll be all right, I suppose.
   C I'm looking forward to seeing you as well.

2 **A** I'd love to, I've always played volleyball.
   B I'd rather not do volleyball because I've never played it before.
   C No, I don't want to do volleyball or anything else, thanks.

3 **A** Yes, I'm much better at football than volleyball, so I'll do that.
   B I'd love to do swimming because I really like being in the water.
   C No thanks, I really don't enjoy sport!

4 **A** Chris, can you find out how much doing football costs, please?
   B Can you ask if I have to wear special trainers at the sports club?
   C Yes, can you get me a leaflet about the sports and send it to me?

> **Exam tip**
> The prompts on the right of the letter help you to write a suitable reply. If you want to get a good mark, you need to respond appropriately to all the points, otherwise your letter will not make sense. Number the points and cross them out when you have included them in your answer. ✓

6 Your teacher will show you a reply to Chris's letter. For each prompt, underline the sentence which directly answers it, and put a wavy line under the sentences that 'expand' it (give extra information). You always need to expand at least two of the points.

Exam task

Now write your own reply to Chris's letter.
Remember to:
- read everything carefully so you understand the whole situation.
- decide what response is needed to the prompts.
- expand on at least two of the prompts.
- check your answer when you have finished.
- write between 120 and 150 words.

> **Exam tip**
> The layout of letters and emails is different, but the technique is the same. Both the situation and the language used will tell you whether a letter is formal or informal. ✓

W *See page 86*

5 Learning

READING Ambitions and achievements

Part 3

1 Some of the words below have similar meanings. Work in pairs. Choose one word to match each of the dictionary definitions.

> adventurous capable cheerful communicative
> competitive creative decisive easygoing
> energetic sympathetic thorough

1 understanding and caring about other people's feelings

2 willing to try new, difficult and often exciting things

3 having imagination or original ideas

4 wanting very much to win or be more successful than others

5 willing to talk to people and give them information

6 able to do things effectively and skilfully and achieve results

2 Look at these photos. Which jobs are shown?

3 What kind of personality do you need to have in order to be good at these jobs? For each photo, choose some of the adjectives in Exercise 1. Then think of some more adjectives for each.

Exam task

You are going to read a magazine article about talented young people. For questions 1–15, choose from the people (A–E). The people may be chosen more than once.

Exam tip

Read text A, go through the questions and find all the A answers. Repeat for texts B-E. Finally, go back and look for any missing answers. ✓

Which person

combined two interests into a possible career? **1** ☐

wants to offer support to others in a similar situation? **2** ☐

knows it will be necessary to keep their knowledge up to date? **3** ☐

went through a period of being occupied with a different interest? **4** ☐

was unsure of the extent of their ability at one stage? **5** ☐

has always used their talent to help them escape from daily life? **6** ☐

realised that they had to take advantage of any opportunity that was offered? **7** ☐

felt at first that they might succeed in a number of different creative areas? **8** ☐

admires others because of their characteristics rather than their achievements? **9** ☐

knows an early interest in their subject allowed them to progress faster? **10** ☐

was initially inspired by the achievements of another person of their own age? **11** ☐

was unaware that it was possible to make a career out of their interest? **12** ☐

came to a sudden decision about what they wanted to do as a job? **13** ☐

thinks it is an advantage to stand out from others when young? **14** ☐

says they come across successful people who look down on others? **15** ☐

My Ambition

We interviewed five talented young people who are already on the way to successful careers.

A Laura

Laura Stanley is only 15 and has already produced an impressive collection of poems and short stories. Her interest in writing started at about eight years old when a girl in her class read aloud a story that she had written. Laura was very impressed by it and decided to have a go herself. She used to sing solos in the school choir and was also an accomplished artist and dancer. For a long time she thought she might follow one of those paths as a career rather than writing, as at the time she didn't really know whether she was good enough at writing. But in the end she has decided that writing is what she loves. 'I know that other kids think I'm weird sometimes because I'd rather be writing than out doing things but it's no bad thing to be a bit different at this stage. You don't get anywhere unless you're different.'

B Haruki

Haruki Kato is a highly dedicated young sculptor. At the age of 16, he has already had his work displayed in galleries and won several competitions. He says he's always sculpted: 'For me it's a way of losing myself in a fantasy world, of cutting everything else out.' He says he's inspired not by successful artists, but by anyone who is driven and determined to get where they want. 'I have a lot of people around me who have helped me and made sure I improve and grow as an artist. In the future, I'd like to do the same for children like me who have a talent but need encouragement so they don't give up. If I weren't studying for exams, I'd spend some of my time teaching them now.'

C Michael

Michael Miller is a 16-year-old magician with big dreams. He has already appeared on TV once. Like many children, he was fascinated by magic tricks when very small and spent hours teaching himself tricks from a little book he was given. 'If I hadn't done that, I wouldn't have had such an advantage when I did start taking it seriously.' However, when he was about twelve he went off magic completely as he spent all his time playing football. Then his brother showed him a new TV programme featuring a magician and he was hooked. He says, 'I do have a lot of ambition. A famous magician says in one of his books that it's good to have big dreams but you don't have to tell anyone your dream. I take his advice so I'll keep my dream to myself for now.'

D Elena

Elena Mancini is a 16-year-old make-up artist with plans for the future. She's already working in local theatres and has even helped on a film set. 'I used to watch my mum putting her make-up on every day and would beg her to put it on me. But for ages I didn't realise that you could do this as a job so I tried to make myself enjoy science as my parents are both scientists.' Elena knows it's a demanding job. 'If I want to do well, I'll have to work very hard. The make-up world is always changing so it's necessary to constantly be learning new techniques.'

E Joel

Joel Bailey, who is 15, wants to be a music journalist and he has already had some interviews published in music magazines. 'For ages, I really didn't know what I wanted to do after school. But I'm a big fan of rock music and I read all the music magazines when I can get hold of them. I enjoy writing as well, and one day I just came up with the idea that I could be a journalist and specialise in music. So I started writing articles and sending them off to magazines. Some I didn't even get paid for, but I didn't mind, because if you want to succeed in any business, you have to get recognised and learn your skills. The only thing I don't like about the music business is that you come across some people who are very arrogant because they feel they are better than the rest of us.'

USE OF ENGLISH

English langua
gram·
way th ...nten
constr
these f
English
features

Part 1

Vocabulary – Phrasal verbs

1 In Use of English Part 1 you often need to choose which phrasal verb fits into a gap. Look back at the texts on page 39 and underline these verbs in the different sections.

give up (B)   go off (C)   come up with (E)   come across (E)

2 It is often possible to guess the meaning of phrasal verbs from the words around them, even if you haven't seen them before. Match the phrasal verbs in Exercise 1 with these meanings.

1 think of
2 stop liking something
3 meet by chance
4 stop doing something

> **Exam tip**
>
> Questions 2, 3 and 6 in the Exam task test phrasal verbs. You will find more practice of these verbs on pages 22 and 24 of the Workbook.

Exam task

For questions 1–12 read the text below and decide which answer (A, B, C or D) best fits each gap. There is an example at the beginning (0).

How my dream came true!

I was born in Pakistan, a country with a vivid history and **(0)** ...D... traditions. Despite loving my country, from **(1)** .... childhood I had dreamt of travelling abroad. Over time, that dream became a firm goal; I wanted to go and live and study in the USA. I decided I had to **(2)** .... a way of persuading my family to move there. Then, when I was fourteen and had almost given **(3)** .... the idea of going to the USA, my father **(4)** .... announced that we were actually moving there!

I quickly **(5)** .... to the American way of life because I'd learnt a lot about the country from the films and books I'd **(6)** .... Although there were still certain things that weren't at all **(7)** .... to me, I didn't suffer much from culture shock. **(8)** ...., I worked hard to form new friendships and fit in at school, things I eventually **(9)** .... to do. In Pakistan they often say that a person should be judged not **(10)** .... by his past achievements but also by his dreams. I'm seventeen now and I have new ambitions. I want to become a doctor, to **(11)** .... a family of my own and to go back to work in Pakistan. I'm sure that if I work hard, I shall have no difficulty in **(12)** .... those goals.

0	A elderly	B antique	C past	D ancient
1	A little	B early	C first	D young
2	A go over	B come down with	C come up with	D go through
3	A up	B away	C back	D out
4	A carelessly	B unexpectedly	C accidentally	D undoubtedly
5	A suited	B altered	C matched	D adapted
6	A kept to	B come across	C gone into	D put up with
7	A common	B usual	C familiar	D frequent
8	A Preferably	B Alternatively	C Otherwise	D Instead
9	A coped	B succeeded	C managed	D handed
10	A quite	B much	C even	D only
11	A keep	B have	C make	D hold
12	A achieving	B obtaining	C performing	D acquiring

Part 4

Grammar – Conditionals

3 Complete these conditional sentences, then check your answers with the reading texts on page 39.

1 If I weren't studying for exams, I .... some of my time teaching them now.
2 If I hadn't done that, I .... such an advantage when I did start taking it seriously.
3 If I want to do well, I .... work very hard.
4 If you want to succeed in any business, you .... get recognised.

4 Which sentence in Exercise 3 is about:

a past events which can't be changed or didn't happen?
b something which is likely in the future?
c something which is impossible or unlikely?
d something which is a general statement of fact?

5 Read the examples and then complete the definitions below with the underlined expressions.

You can go to the beach <u>providing (that) / provided (that)</u> you finish your homework.

Tom will come swimming <u>as / so long as</u> he finishes his homework in time.

I'll bring my coat <u>in case</u> it rains.

We'll go to the beach <u>unless</u> it rains.

1 .... means the same as *except if*.
2 .... means *because it's possible something might happen*.
3 .... and .... mean the same as *only if* or *on condition that*.

6 Choose the correct expression in these sentences.

1 I'll come to the film *unless / as long as* there's a match on TV I want to watch.
2 I won't come to the film *if / unless* there's a match on TV I want to watch.
3 Take some money *unless / in case* you need to get the bus home.
4 I'll lend you some money *in case / so long as* you give it back tomorrow.

G *See page 82*

Exam task

In Use of English Part 4 there are eight sentences to be rewritten. There are five in the task below.

For questions 1–5, complete the second sentence so it has a similar meaning to the first sentence, using the word given. Do not change the word given. You must use between two and five words, including the word given.

> **Exam tip**
>
> The sentence you write needs to include the word in capitals and to be grammatically correct. It must also have the same meaning as the first sentence. ✓

0 I suddenly thought of how I could persuade my mum to let me go on the trip.
CAME
I suddenly *came up with a* way of persuading my mum to let me go on the trip.

1 I don't think we'll be chosen for the team because we're not practising enough.
UNLESS
We won't be chosen for the team .... more.

2 I'll come to the party if you let my sister come too.
PROVIDED
I'll come to the party .... allowed to come too.

3 The museum might not have a café so we need to take a packed lunch.
CASE
We need to take a packed lunch .... a café in the museum.

4 I regret not having done any revision, but I didn't know the test was today.
HAVE
If I had known the test was today, I .... revision.

5 To be good at a sport, you have to do several hours of practice every day.
NEED
If you want to be good at a sport, you .... several hours every day.

5 LISTENING   Education

Part 2

1 Work in pairs. Make sentences about yourself with some of these words.

primary school ☐   head ☐   secondary school ☐   attend ☐   state ☐
comprehensive ☐   streamed ☐   set ☐   uniform ☐   sports kit ☐   lessons ☐
pupils ☐   playing fields ☐   canteen ☐   laboratories ☐   library ☐
swimming pool ☐   teacher ☐   classes ☐   timetable ☐   homework ☐   rules ☐

2 🔊 **1.13** Now listen to Anna, an English girl, talking about her education. Tick (✔) the words from Exercise 1 she uses.

3 Anna used these words on the recording. Match the underlined words in the sentences in Exercise 4 with a word below which has the same meaning.

> attended   catching   highest group   put on

4 🔊 **1.13** Now listen to the recording again and complete the gaps with one or two words.

1 Anna <u>went to</u> a .... school very close to her home.
2 Anna is in the <u>top set</u> for ....
3 Anna had to <u>wear</u> a white polo shirt and .... for sports lessons.
4 Anna found <u>getting</u> the .... difficult because she wasn't used to it.

5 Work in groups of three or four to answer these questions.

1 Anna has attended state schools. Is the school you are at a state school or a private one?
2 Anna's secondary school is *comprehensive* (anyone can go to it). Do children have to take an exam to get a place in your school or can anyone go?
3 Subjects at Anna's school are *streamed*. Are children at your school divided into groups or sets for different subjects according to their ability? Is this a good idea?
4 Anna's school has good *facilities*, like playing fields and a canteen. Are the facilities at your school good?

Exam tip

The words you hear before (or occasionally after) you hear the answer in the recording will be very similar to the words in the question, but not identical. ✓

6 Work in pairs. Discuss these questions about educational visits.

What is an educational visit? What sort of places do you go to on an educational visit? Have you been on any educational visits with your class/school? Where did you go?

7 You are going to hear a boy talking about a class educational visit. Look at the photos. What do you think he saw there? Write down five words you think you might hear in the talk.

8 Now look at the underlined words in the Exam task below. Match them with words in the box with the same meaning. You will hear these words in the recording.

amazed   building   built   came to a close   defended
described   didn't appear   hard   not far from   press

Exam task

🔊 1.14 You will hear a student called Max talking about his visit to the Aeroseum in Gothenberg, Sweden. For questions 1–10, complete the sentences.

VISIT TO THE AEROSEUM

The museum is built <u>very close to</u> an old [**1**] and situated in some underground shelters.

During the <u>construction</u> of the shelters, a lot of [**2**] had to be moved.

The shelters <u>could not be found</u> on [**3**] after they were built, so for years no one knew about them.

To enter the museum, you have to <u>push</u> a [**4**] by the main doors.

The main doors were made very thick so they <u>could protect</u> everything from [**5**] .

Max was <u>surprised</u> to see some [**6**] which looked very modern just inside the museum.

Max thought the pilot would have found the [**7**] of the cabin <u>difficult</u> to deal with.

Max preferred listening to a volunteer who <u>talked about</u> [**8**] and flying planes.

Max enjoyed watching some people covering a wing <u>made</u> of [**9**] .

Max's visit <u>ended</u> in the [**10**] room.

9 Work in pairs. Did you get all the answers right? If not, what mistakes did you make?

A I spelled the word wrong. Questions ....
B I wrote the wrong answer. Questions ....
C I got lost and missed the answer. Questions ....

Exam tip

The first possible answer you hear will not necessarily be the correct one. Some words are there to distract you! ✔

5 SPEAKING

Vocabulary – School subjects

1 Tick (✔) the subjects you are studying, then compare with a partner.

English ☐   other foreign languages ☐
my own language and literature ☐
maths ☐   science ☐   history ☐
geography ☐   IT ☐   sport ☐
art ☐   music ☐   drama ☐

other subjects: ....

2 Tell your partner which of the subjects in Exercise 1 you like best. Use reasons a–e to explain why.

  a I'm good at it.
  b The teacher's great.
  c It's an interesting subject.
  d It'll be useful.
  e Other: ....

Part 1

3 Match the speech bubbles with the questions then, in pairs, ask and answer them. Remember to add some extra information.

A   I'd love to learn Chinese if I could.

B   I hope to pass all my exams and go to university.

C   I'd like to be a scientist if I get good grades.

D   How to sit still!

Ambitions and achievements
1 What job would you like to do when you grow up?
2 What do you expect to achieve in the next five years?
Education
3 What was the most important thing you learned at primary school?
4 Is there a new subject you'd really like to study?

Part 2

4 Work in pairs and do the task below.

> **Candidate A:** Look at photographs A and B. Compare them and answer the question. Tell your answer to Candidate B. Use these phrases if you are not sure about what you see in the photo: *it may/might/could be a ...*   *it looks like a ...* *it's similar to a ...*   *it's a sort of ...*
>
> **Candidate B:** When Candidate A has finished, discuss together which lesson you would prefer to do and why. Give reasons. Here are some phrases you can use:
> *I'd rather ... because it's more interesting.*   *It's good to learn something new.*   *I'd rather be outside.*   *I don't like/enjoy doing ... because ...*

Exam tip

Don't worry if you don't know a particular word, or if you are unsure what you can see in the photographs! Keep talking and make intelligent guesses using the phrases above. ✔

What might pupils learn by doing these different subjects at school?

What do you think the pupils will learn on their visits?

Exam task

Now do the same with photographs C and D. Candidate B should start. Use the phrases in Exercise 4 to help you. When Candidate B has finished, discuss which of the visits you would prefer to go on and why.

5 WRITING

Part 2: Report

1 Read the exam question and a candidate's report below. Work in pairs. Are these sentences true or false?

The candidate:
1 has answered both parts of the question.
2 has used suitable headings in his report.
3 thinks the teaching at his school is poor.
4 feels he is too old to wear school uniform.
5 has used an appropriate style.

> Your teacher has asked you to write a report for homework saying what you like most about your school and what change(s) you would recommend. Write your report. (Use 120–180 words.)

> ### Report on my school
>
> #### Introduction
> I'm very (1) <u>lucky</u> because I'm happy at my secondary school, which is good because I have to study here for another five years.
>
> #### What I like most about my school
> I (2) <u>do</u> a lot of sport, which I enjoy very much. (3) <u>And</u> I appreciate the fact that there are playing fields right outside. (4) <u>Where</u> lessons <u>are concerned</u>, my favourite subject is history, and I have a really (5) <u>fab</u> history teacher called Mr Peterson. The teachers are enthusiastic about their subjects and (6) <u>so</u> the lessons are well taught.
>
> #### The changes I would recommend
> I suggest the head should (7) <u>get rid of</u> school uniform. (8) <u>When</u> you're 13 or 14, you don't like wearing the same clothes as everyone else! I'd also recommend giving everyone one night a week without homework. We get really tired studying all the time, and (9) <u>in my view</u>, we would concentrate better on other days if we had at least one night free to relax!
>
> #### Conclusion
> My school is already (10) <u>great</u>, but making a few changes would keep the pupils happy!

> **Exam tip**
>
> You will get a better mark for your report if you use headings for each section. A report should be formal or semi-formal in style.

2 Match these more formal words and phrases with the ones underlined in the text.

a by the time
b abolish
c therefore
d in addition
e impressive
f take part in
g very good
h in my opinion
i as for
j fortunate

3 You are often asked to make suggestions or recommendations in a report. Underline the three examples in the report on the left, and then complete these sentences with your own ideas.

1 I suggest that my school should build a new ... because ...
2 I recommend introducing ... at my school because ...
3 In my view ... because ...

Exam task

Now write the answer to one of these questions.

1 Your teacher has asked you to write a report for homework saying which new subject you would like to study at school and why.
2 You have been on a class visit to a museum. Now your teacher has asked you to write a report on the visit, explaining what you learned and whether you would recommend the visit to other pupils.

Remember to:
- plan your report before you begin.
- use vocabulary and structures from the unit.
- decide what your introduction and headings will be.
- use a formal or semi-formal style.
- make sure you use the correct number of words.

W *See page 89*

6 Natural world

LISTENING

Environment and weather

Part 4

A

B

C

D

1 Work in pairs. Which photo shows these things, A, B, C or D? (Some may be in more than one photo.)

bushes   grass   grey sky   lakes   mountains
pine trees   rocks   snow and ice   sunshine   volcanoes

2 Now match the photos with these countries. What helped you to decide?

Australia   Cameroon   Canada   Iceland

3 🔵 1.15 You will hear three teenagers each talking about the weather and environment in one of the countries above. Which country does each speaker talk about?

Speaker 1 ....   Speaker 2 ....   Speaker 3 ....

Which words gave you the answer?

4 🔵 1.15 Listen again and make a list of the adjectives, nouns and expressions the speakers use to describe the weather.

Adjectives	Nouns	Expressions
mild	sunshine	
		temperatures below zero

5 Tick (✔) the words and expressions that can be used about your country. In pairs, talk about the weather in your country. What is your favourite time of year? Why?

6 Which countries in the box have the problems below? Work in pairs or small groups. You can find the information on the internet or in a book if you need to.

Bangladesh Brazil Italy Jamaica Saudi Arabia Spain Switzerland the USA

forests disappearing .....Brazil......
volcanoes erupting ....
industrial pollution ....
rivers drying up ....
lack of rain ....
flooding ....
hurricanes ....
snow and ice melting ....

Do you have any of these problems in your country? What can be done about them?

Grammar – Countable and uncountable nouns

7 *River* is a countable noun and *pollution* is an uncountable noun. Answer these questions about countable and uncountable nouns.

1 Which kind of noun can be singular or plural?
2 Which kind of noun cannot be plural and takes a singular verb?

8 Write the nouns from Exercises 1, 4 and 6 into the correct list.

Countable	Uncountable
river	pollution

 See page 83

Exam task

Exam tip

If you find a question difficult, listen for words which tell you which of the possible answers are wrong. This will make it easier to choose the correct one.

🔊 **1.16** You will hear a boy called Tim talking to his teacher about a school project he has done on the environment. For questions 1–7, choose the best answer (A, B or C).

1 Why did Tim choose to do a project on the environment?
  A His family persuaded him to take part.
  B He wanted to take positive action.
  C He was interested in the scientific issues.

2 What change has Tim made in his travel habits?
  A He walks to school rather than taking the bus.
  B He catches the bus to school rather than travelling by car.
  C He cycles to school instead of getting a lift.

3 What suggestion will Tim make about paper use at school?
  A Students should use only paper that has been recycled.
  B Students should avoid using paper when submitting work.
  C Students should use both sides of paper whenever possible.

4 What improvement does Tim propose for the school cafeteria?
  A getting rid of drinks machines
  B making the menu vegetarian
  C purchasing food grown locally

5 Tim thinks that all young people should
  A study in natural light whenever possible.
  B turn off electrical equipment they're not using.
  C try to avoid using air conditioning.

6 What does Tim say about using water?
  A Even small actions can reduce water use.
  B An international solution is needed for water shortages.
  C Some people refuse to try and save water.

7 What does Tim believe families should do when shopping?
  A avoid buying expensive ready meals
  B refuse to pay for unnecessary plastic bags
  C reduce the amount of packaged food they buy

9 Now your teacher will show you what Tim said. In pairs, look at the recording script for each question, and underline the words that give you the answer. Then highlight the words that show you the other answers are wrong.

Exam tip

The answers will be in the same order as the questions, so keep listening even if you miss an answer.

6 SPEAKING

Part 3

1 In Speaking Part 3, the examiner introduces the topic, shows you some pictures and asks you to talk about the two questions written above them. Make notes of what you could say about these pictures.

- How successful would these suggestions for helping the environment be?
- Which two would be the best to choose and why?

2 You should have a discussion about the pictures. You can agree, disagree, make a comment or a suggestion using the phrases in the speech bubbles. Write A, D, C or S next to each speech bubble.

1 I don't really think that's a good idea.

2 Absolutely.

3 We all know we shouldn't drop litter.

4 We could tell everyone to turn off their computers at the end of the lesson.

5 I don't think making a wildlife area would go down well with students here.

6 I'm with you on that.

7 That's not what I think, I'm afraid.

8 What about getting recycling bins in the canteen?

Exam task

Now practise doing the task with your partner. Make sure you answer the two questions above the pictures.

> **Exam tip**
>
> You have three minutes to discuss the two questions. Start speaking straight away. Cooperate with your partner and ask him/her to respond, e.g. *What do you think? Do you agree? And you?* ✓

Part 4

Exam task

The examiner will ask you some general questions related to Part 3. You have four minutes to complete Part 4 in the exam. Take it in turns to ask and answer the questions below with your partner.

- Do students at your school do any of the things shown in the pictures? Which ones?
- Do you think your school is environmentally friendly? Why? / Why not?
- Do you think young people care about the environment more than older people? Why? / Why not?
- What kind of things do you and your family do at home to help the environment?
- Why is it important to do things like recycling?

6

WRITING

Part 2: Article

1 You may be asked to write an article on a very wide range of subjects. You don't always have to be very serious, but you do need to get the reader's attention and keep it. Which of these strategies will help you to do this?

1 asking questions to involve the reader
2 making an amusing comment
3 using long and complicated words
4 finishing in a memorable way
5 making lots of comparisons
6 giving personal examples

2 This article was written for a school magazine. Read it and find examples of the helpful strategies in Exercise 1. Highlight them in different colours.

What I do to be 'green' at home and at school

We all have to do something to help the environment, don't we? I'm only 14 though, so there's no way I personally can do anything about the really big problems, like climate change, is there?
However, I can make sure I live my own life in a green way. At home that means not taking baths, because they use too much hot water. (Don't worry, I still take showers!) I turn off the lights and heating in my room when I leave, so I don't waste electricity. I'm very green when it comes to transport too, because I walk everywhere. When I go out with my family we often take the train rather than the car, especially if we want to go into the city, because it's quicker and cheaper.
At school, I help to collect and recycle all the rubbish. That involves collecting everything from the cafeteria. Our head teacher has also decided to turn the central heating on a month later than usual. It's OK, I've put my jumper on!
So I can honestly say that I'm as green as I can be. Are you?

3 Compare your answers with a partner and then answer these questions.

Is this article written in a formal, semi-formal or informal style? Is this appropriate? Why? Can you think of any different ways to end the article?

4 Here is part of another article. Complete the main paragraph with some of the underlined words and phrases in the article in Exercise 2.

My favourite time of year

Why is that? Most of all **(1)** .... school has finished and that **(2)** .... going to the beach with my friends, relaxing on the warm sand, swimming and snorkelling. **(3)** .... eating out, we often go and eat at a little restaurant on the beach, **(4)** .... we want to meet my aunt and my cousins. We always spend the evenings there too; when it's warm, the stars are shining and the music is playing, it's absolute magic. Wouldn't anyone love this experience? For me summer **(5)** .... not having any stress or pressure, relaxing and enjoying the sunshine. **(6)** ...., it also **(7)** .... getting together with family and relations, some of whom I don't see during the rest of the year.

5 Now write out the article, giving it a good introduction and a memorable ending. Try to put a question in the introduction, and add an amusing comment to the main paragraph.

Exam task

Do one of the following tasks for homework (120–180 words).

A Your teacher has asked you to write an article for the school magazine with the title:
What I love and hate about the weather in my country.

B You have seen this announcement on a teenage website:

Articles wanted!
Do you have problems with the environment and pollution in your country?
Write and tell us about them, **and** say whether you think these problems can be solved.
The best articles will be posted on the website next month.

Write your **article.**

Remember to:
• give your article a title.
• begin with an interesting introduction.
• involve your reader with questions.
• use your own knowledge and experience.
• try to end it in an amusing or interesting way.

 See page 90

6 READING Wildlife

1 Work in pairs. What are these animals and where can you find them?

2 In what ways are these animals different from each other? Think about where they live, what they look like and what they eat. Use a dictionary to help you if necessary.

> A lives in the jungle but C lives in the ocean.

> ... and B lives on grassland, in Africa, I think.

3 Do the three animals have anything in common? If so, what?

4 Read this short text and the sentences which follow. Underline the differences between the three sentences. Which sentence fits best in the gap?

> Elephants' huge ears are capable of detecting all kinds of noises which a human cannot hear. .... There is a wide range of these that can travel huge distances and are picked up not just by other elephants' ears but also by the soles of their feet.

A Because of this, the sounds the animals produce are even more impressive.

B Therefore, the sounds the animals produce are even more impressive.

C The sounds the animals produce, however, are even more impressive.

> **Exam tip**
>
> Words and expressions like *however, though, because of this* and *therefore* help you decide if a sentence follows the argument in a text and fits in a gap. Read before and after the gap.

You are going to read an article about the 'singing' of humpback whales. Seven sentences have been removed from the article. Choose from the sentences A–H the one which fits each gap. There is one extra sentence that you do not need to use.

Even humpback whales have hit songs!

The fact that male humpback whales sing long, sweet melodies has been known for many years. However, a new finding suggests that some melodies become so popular that they are sung by whales all over the world!

But before we look further into this exciting discovery, here is a bit of background about the tunes sung by these mammals. Unlike the songs released as records by humans, which last for three or four minutes, these soulful whale songs last for ten to twenty minutes. **1** [ ] Scientists are not sure whether they sing to attract females or to ward off competitors, but apparently once they begin, the mammals sing the same song over and over, for 24 hours at a time.

Also, they 'release' a new song every year which can be totally original. **2** [ ] What is really interesting though about this 'song of the year' is that while scientists have known for some time that it is sung by the entire population of male whales that live in one group (known as a pod), they recently discovered that it was also 'downloaded' by whales that lived in other areas of the world.

This new research was conducted by University of Queensland biologists Ellen Garland and Michael Noad, who recorded songs from six different Pacific whale populations over a number of years. What they observed is amazing. In almost every case, the annual songs originated from a pod of humpback whales off Australia's eastern coast. **3** [ ]

One such song became such a super hit that it travelled all the way to the Atlantic! However, since they don't have iTunes or iPods, this process takes about two years.

The scientists are not yet sure whether the songs were passed on by humpbacks who moved from one pod to another, or were shared by the different populations when they met while they were migrating from one area to another. **4** [ ] This is something that has never been observed before in the animal kingdom and in this respect they are very similar to humans.

The East Australian whale population is one of the largest in the Pacific. **5** [ ] Whales are very mobile animals who can swim hundreds of miles per day and their song carries well underwater so a large group of whales can spread it over a wide area.

Since they are amongst the largest species of whales, humpbacks are easy to spot. **6** [ ] These incredible mammals can dive up to 45 minutes, reach depths of 180 metres and see underwater for more than 120 metres. They can blow bubbles from their blowholes on the top of their heads at speeds exceeding 450 kilometres per hour and have lungs large enough to hold nearly 10,000 litres of air. **7** [ ] Their famous songs, which can be heard for over 160 kilometres, are 'sung' by blowing air through their blowholes. The one sad part is that there are currently only about 10,000 of these wonderful creatures left.

A Their most amazing feature though is that they have no vocal cords.

B However, the finding is considered very important, because it confirms that whales exchange their culture with each other.

C And they are not just random noises, but are made of actual themes that keep repeating and developing.

D More often than not though, it is actually a remix of a previous one.

E Because of this, these whales seem to have more influence on what songs are taken up.

F Therefore they appeared to stay still for some time in one geographical location while they did this.

G This is also thanks to the unique markings on the underside of their tail.

H The same song would move from group to group, until it was being sung by whales about 4,000 miles away.

5 Work in pairs to discuss the following.

1 When you have finished the task, compare your answers with a partner. If you disagree on an answer, look at the question again, and see if you can work out who is right.

2 What will you do in the exam if you are unable to answer a question?

3 What is the writer comparing the whales to in this text? Why?

6 USE OF ENGLISH

Part 2

Grammar – Articles

1 Put the correct words into the rules about articles.

> *a* *an* *the* no article

We use ...

1 .... or .... with singular uncountable nouns that introduce a new item of information.
2 .... with countable and uncountable nouns, when the item has been mentioned before.
3 .... + noun when the speaker and listener both know what they are talking about.
4 .... with uncountable and plural countable nouns when we talk about things in a general sense.
5 .... with the names of most buildings, cities, countries, lakes, towns, villages and mountains.
6 .... with the names of certain countries (with the word *kingdom*, *republic* or *state*), regions, deserts, mountain ranges, oceans, rivers and seas.

2 Which of these place names need *the* before them? Write them next to the correct heading.

> Atlantic Ocean   California   Czech Republic
> Far East   Himalayas   Italy   Lake Como
> London   Nile   North of England   Sahara
> South America   Thames   United Kingdom
> United States

Oceans, seas and rivers: the...............................
Regions: the..
Countries: the...
Deserts and mountain ranges: the.....................

Add some more examples to the lists if you can.

3 ⊙ Complete these sentences with *a* or *the*.

1 I heard .... strange noise coming from downstairs in .... kitchen.
2 Julie wanted .... cold drink but there were no drinks left in .... fridge.
3 We wanted to catch .... bus to .... airport, but there were none that left early enough.
4 They learned .... words of .... new song in class yesterday.
5 I really enjoyed reading .... book you lent me.

4 Which sentences need *the* and which no article? Complete them with *the* or leave a gap.

1 All the pupils at my school study .... geography.
2 We studied .... geography of India in class yesterday.
3 I gave my sister .... money I owed her.
4 My grandparents say that .... money doesn't always make you happy.

5 Complete the text with *a*, *an*, *the* or leave a gap for no article.

Some interesting facts about the weather and climate

- Recent increases in temperatures across **(1)** .... world have been linked to human activity, such as **(2)** .... burning of fossil fuels like **(3)** .... oil and coal. Global warming has become **(4)** .... important issue for governments everywhere as they try to find **(5)** .... way to deal with **(6)** .... effects of climate change.

- The hottest temperature ever recorded was 57.8°C in **(7)** .... Libya in September 1922. **(8)** .... coldest was at Vostok Station in **(9)** .... Antarctica in July 1983.

- The highest rainfall ever recorded in 24 hours was 182.5 cm in La Réunion, during **(10)** .... Hurricane Denise in January 1966. The most rainfall ever recorded in one year was 25.4 m in **(11)** .... India.

- The highest snowfall ever recorded in **(12)** .... one-year period was 31.1 m in **(13)** .... Washington State, in 1972.

- **(14)** .... USA also has more tornadoes than any other country, averaging around 1200 each year.

- **(15)** .... water covers 70% of **(16)** .... Earth's surface, the three largest oceans being **(17)** .... Pacific, **(18)** .... Atlantic and **(19)** .... Indian Ocean. The longest river in the world is **(20)** .... Nile, which is 6,650 km in length.

G *See page 83*

Grammar – *so* and *such* (*a/an*)

6 Complete the sentences with *so* or *such*.

1 The Siberian tiger is .... a rare animal that few people have seen one.
2 The recycling campaign was .... well-organised that everyone took part.
3 The students responded with .... enthusiasm to the idea of 'adopting' an animal at the zoo that the teacher organised it at once.
4 The talk about the rainforest was attended by .... a lot of people that there weren't enough chairs.
5 Plans to build a new motorway were dropped because .... many people objected.
6 The deer ran away .... rapidly that the lion couldn't catch it.

Now complete the rules.

We use .... with nouns (with or without an adjective) and the expression *a lot* (*of*).
We use .... with an adjective or adverb, and the words *many*, *much* and *few*.

too and *enough*

7 Write a sentence about each cartoon using *too* or *enough* and one of these words.

big food money steep

G *See page 83*

G *See page 83*

Exam task

For questions 1–12, read the text below and think of the word which best fits each gap. Use only one word in each gap. There is an example at the beginning (0).

Lala the Penguin

You might think all penguins **(0)** ...*have*... to live somewhere really cold like Antarctica, but not Lala. This fourteen-year-old King Penguin not **(1)** .... lives in Japan, but is also a household pet.

Lala's path to domestic life began about ten years **(2)** ...., after he was accidentally caught in a fisherman's net. He was **(3)** .... sick to swim away so he was rescued and nursed back to health by a family. However, **(4)** .... they tried to return him to the water, Lala refused to leave, so **(5)** .... family decided to adopt him instead, and installed him in a giant room with air conditioning in their home. Lala lives in **(6)** .... comfort today that he wanders around the family property looking and acting **(7)** .... a king!

If **(8)** .... is one thing Lala likes more than his cool and pleasant accommodation, **(9)** .... is his daily shopping trip to town. He waddles off **(10)** .... morning with a penguin-shaped backpack. His first and only stop is at the local fish store, **(11)** .... he gets two fish, his daily dose of protein. He eats one fish in the shop and puts the **(12)** .... inside his backpack.

The funny thing is, the people of the town are so used to seeing him now that nobody takes any notice!

8 Check your answers with a partner. If you disagree, explain to each other why your answer is right or wrong.

7

People and style
LISTENING   Shopping and fashion

Part 3

Ⓐ

Ⓑ

Ⓒ

1 Work in pairs. Choose three of the adjectives and expressions to describe the clothes in each photo.

casual colourful comfortable cool designer clothes elegant everyday expensive-looking formal individual outrageous second-hand smart sports clothes stylish unfashionable vintage well-designed

2 Discuss these questions in a group.

1 Do you ever dress like the people in the photographs? When?
2 What are your favourite clothes?
3 Do you prefer to wear the same clothes as your friends or to look different?
4 Do you think you can tell someone's personality from their clothes?

3 🔘 1.17 Listen to one of the people in the photos. In pairs, answer these questions.

1 Which person is speaking?
2 Is he/she like you?
3 Do you know anyone like this?

4 🔘 1.17 The expressions below are different from those the speaker uses but they have a similar meaning. Try to remember and write some of the words she uses. Then listen again and write the rest.

1 be passionate about
2 staying in touch with
3 look different
4 clothes which are slightly shocking
5 clothes which are fairly typical
6 look good on me
7 becomes unfashionable
8 get rid of
9 become fashionable again
10 be very rich
11 draw attention to yourself
12 clothes by particular designers

Exam task

Exam tip

In Listening Part 3 you need to listen for words and expressions which have similar meanings to those in the questions. ✓

🔘 1.18 You will hear five people talking about shopping for clothes. For questions 1–5, choose from the list (A–F) what each speaker says. Use each letter only once. There is one extra letter which you do not need to use.

A I prefer certain colours.

B I am passionate about the latest fashions.

C I try to stand out from everyone else.

D I know what styles suit me.

E I dress in the same way as my friends.

F I like to look smart.

Speaker 1 ☐☐
Speaker 2 ☐☐
Speaker 3 ☐☐
Speaker 4 ☐☐
Speaker 5 ☐☐

7 SPEAKING

Part 1

1 🔊 **1.19** Listen to two students answering some Part 1 questions and write down what they like and dislike.

	Like	Dislike	Neither like nor dislike
Giulia			
Jorge			

2 🔊 **1.19** Listen again and complete the phrases they use.

Like	Dislike	Neither like nor dislike
I'm .... music. I .... singing. I'm .... football, of course. I .... going to see them … I'm .... skiing. History and geography are	I'm .... playing football myself. I .... playing other sports very much. I'm .... going to the mountains in the summer. I .... going for long walks.	Well, English is OK but it's .... I .... doing science.

Exam task

Work in pairs to ask and answer the questions below. If your partner doesn't have much to say, use the question in brackets to help.

> **Exam tip**
> The examiner will ask you two or three questions about your everyday life, your free time and your school. This will include some questions about what you like.

- Do you prefer watching sports to playing them? (Why?)
- Do you enjoy watching TV? (Tell me about a programme you have watched recently.)
- Do you enjoy reading books? (What kind of books do you like? / Why don't you enjoy reading books?)
- What do you like doing on holiday? (Why do you enjoy it?)

Grammar – Verbs and expressions followed by *to*-infinitive or *-ing* form

3 Giulia and Jorge used these verbs and expressions. Which ones are followed by a *to*-infinitive and which by the *-ing* form of the verb? Put them by the correct heading.

> attempt   can't bear   don't mind
> enjoy   hope   be interested in
> be keen on   like   love   prefer
> want   would like   would prefer

***to*-infinitive**	
***-ing* form**	
either *to*-infinitive or *-ing* form	

4 👁 Exam candidates often make mistakes with verb forms. Choose the correct form in these sentences and put any new verbs into the table in Exercise 3.

1 If you agree *coming* / *to come*, just bring some cold cola, because it'll be hot.
2 I look forward to *seeing* / *see* you at the airport.
3 I hope *see* / *to see* you on Monday!
4 Would you like *come* / *to come* to visit me?
5 I would prefer *going* / *to go* to a film rather than watch TV.
6 I suggested *going* / *to go* for a walk along the beach.
7 I cannot imagine *to live* / *living* in a small village.
8 Your parents don't want you *go* / *to go* somewhere dangerous.
9 I prefer *to buy* / *buy* clothes by myself and with my own money.
10 I love surfing on the net and *playing* / *play* tennis.

G *See page 84*

Part 2

5 These photos show four different ways of shopping.
   Which of the ways would you prefer?

6 🔊 **1.20** Listen to Adam, a student, talking in a speaking exam.
   Which of the photos has Adam been given? Tick (✔) the ideas
   below which he mentions.

Advantages

lots of choice ☐   more unusual stuff for sale ☐

other facilities ☐   compare prices ☐

convenient ☐   you can try clothes on ☐

latest fashions ☐   more fun ☐

Disadvantages

quite traditional ☐   too crowded ☐

not much for teenagers ☐   bad quality ☐

can't try things on ☐   wait for the post ☐

7 Complete the expressions Adam used when
   he didn't know what to say.

   1 Mmm, ... me ....

   2 .... me .... for a ....

   3 Not .... would .... but I think ...

> **Exam tip**
>
> When you need to think, say something in English to
> give yourself time. ✔

8 Work in pairs. Write down other things you could say about the
   photographs Adam talked about.

9 Now look at the other two photographs. Can you use the same
   ideas to talk about these photos? Try to think of some more
   ideas and write them down.

Exam task

Work in pairs. Choose two photographs each and compare
them. Say what the advantages are of shopping in these ways.
Time yourselves and talk for one minute each.

Here are some words you can use to connect your ideas about
the photos:

whereas   on the other hand   the difference is that   in both photos

> **Exam tip**
>
> While your partner is talking, think
> about your own opinion of the
> topic as the examiner will ask you
> a question at the end. You only
> need to say a sentence or two. ✔

7 WRITING | People and feelings

Part 2: Informal letter

1 Read this exam task and the letter from Anna on the right. Work in pairs to complete the letter with the words and phrases in the box below.

You have received this letter from your English friend Lauren.

> … and I'm doing a project at school. We have to find which famous people teenagers admire, and why. Can you choose a famous person you admire and write and tell me why you admire them? It'll be interesting to see who you've chosen!
>
> Thanks for helping me, Lauren

as a result   comes across as despite   even   even though famous for being   managed to nobody could impress me one other quality which the man who

2 Highlight the adjectives Anna used to describe Nelson Mandela's personality in the letter.

3 Which famous person would you write about? Work in pairs and do the following.

1 Tell your partner who you have chosen and why he or she is famous.
2 Tick (✔) any of the adjectives in the letter you can use to describe him or her.
3 Make a note of any other adjectives you want to use below.

4 Write your own answer to Lauren.

Remember to:
- begin and end your letter correctly.
- start by saying who you admire and why.
- explain why the person is famous.
- use some of the adjectives from Exercise 2 in your description of the person.
- use some of the phrases from Exercise 1 to link your ideas together.

Ⓦ See page 90

> Dear Lauren
> You asked me to write and tell you about a famous person I admire. Well, that's easy! (1) .... more than Nelson Mandela!
> He is (2) .... the first black president of South Africa, and for being (3) .... brought freedom to his people. (4) .... spending 27 years in prison, he never got discouraged. He (5) .... keep smiling, stay optimistic and be cheerful. He never, ever gave up. He was amazingly confident and (6) .... of this belief in himself he achieved the most amazing things. (7) .... he was fighting a very cruel system, he was always patient, polite and thoughtful to those around him. He was a lawyer at the start of his career, and (8) .... the wardens in the prison admired him.
> There is (9) .... I really like. If you look at the photos and videos of him, you can see he was always laughing and smiling. There are photos of him dancing and meeting famous singers and film stars when he was president. He loves life and music! He (10) .... such a great guy! I wish I could meet him.
> I hope you like what I've written.
> Best wishes,
> Anna

5 Is there a person in your family you admire, or a student in your school/college? Work in pairs and do the following.

1 Tell your partner who you have chosen and why.
2 Write down any adjectives you can use to describe him/her.
3 Do one of the exam tasks below.

Exam task

Write an answer to one of these exam tasks. Write 120–180 words in an appropriate style.

1 You have received this letter from your Australian friend, Andrew.

> I'm doing a project at school. We have to find out which person in their family teenagers admire, and why. Can you choose one person in your family you admire and write and tell me why?
> Thanks for helping me.
> Andrew

Write your **letter**.

2 You have received this letter from your friend, Julia.

> We're doing a project in our English class. We have to find out which student in their school or college other students admire, and why. Can you choose one student you admire and write and tell me why?
> Thanks.
> Julia

Write your **letter**.

7 READING

1 Read the following text. Tick (✔) the adjectives which describe the writer's feelings. You can tick more than one adjective.

amused ☐   annoyed ☐   angry ☐   ashamed ☐   concerned ☐

curious ☐   furious ☐   guilty ☐   irritated ☐   upset ☐

> As Olivia came into the room, she glanced around in that irritating way she sometimes has, trying to decide if it was worth coming into the crowded room. Then she noticed the birthday cake on the table and obviously decided it was. I was standing with my friends and I looked up and half smiled at her, waiting for her to say 'Hi'. Although I had to move out of her way to let her pass, she turned her head and walked right on with her usual confidence, as if she'd never seen me before, and found a space for herself on the sofa. I carried on talking to my friends and stopped myself going over and telling her what I thought of her. That wouldn't have been a good idea while I was so mad at her!

2 Now answer this exam question about the text.

How did the writer feel?
A irritated that Olivia had arrived at the party so late
B angry that he found it less easy to make friends than Olivia
C annoyed that Olivia deliberately took no notice of him
D upset that he didn't have the confidence to speak to Olivia

Exam tip

Read the whole of each option carefully and check what the text says. Some of the words in an option may be in the text (e.g. *irritate*, *confidence*) but it doesn't mean that option is the right answer. ✓

3 Read the extract below quickly to get an idea of what it is about. Ask yourself questions while you read: Who? Why? Where? How are people in the text feeling?

4 Work in pairs to discuss your answers.

Exam task

You are going to read an extract from a novel about a girl who has just moved to live in a new place. For questions 1–8, choose the answer (A, B, C or D) which you think fits best according to the text.

The very first time I saw Andy Byron, I was wandering about in the autumnal woods below my new home and thinking about my lonely fate, so when I realised that I wasn't actually alone, I felt cheated. What was this boy doing, cluttering up the picturesque scene? There he stood on the wooden bridge at the foot of the hill, leaning on the rail and completely blocking my way across.

Of course, I didn't have to cross the river. I could go back to the new house in time for Mum's return from the shops, but I wasn't going to let some boy prevent me from exploring my new surroundings. So I hurried down the hill and onto the bridge. He barely looked at me, and moved over just enough for me to get past. I stamped on, my tatty old trainers slapping against the boards, and then swung right, as though I knew where I was going.

In fact, there was a path alongside the river, probably full of joggers and cyclists at weekends, but completely empty on a sunny weekday morning like this one. Nobody for miles around except for me and the boy on the bridge. And anyway, what was he doing here? I had the day off school in order to help Mum with the move, but what was his excuse? Despite myself, I slowed down as the path meandered through a group of what even I recognised as birch trees, and glanced back. And precisely as I did so, he looked up and our eyes met. I was so furious with myself that I turned sharply away, but even before I'd turned, he had dropped his gaze back to the water.

But the incident brought back the bad temper against which I'd been struggling all day. I'd just been telling myself that I didn't really mind moving out here from Edinburgh, and that the autumn leaves were actually quite pretty, and the very first person I meet is this hateful boy! I sat down on a big stone and stared gloomily into the river. It was just fate that I'd been dragged away from all my friends and brought here to the end of the bus route. I couldn't even blame Mum and Dad so I leaned my head on my hands in order to feel sorry for myself more effectively, but I caught sight of my watch as ___line 39___ I did so and jumped to my feet. Midday! Mum would be back now with her load of scrubbing brushes and cleaning products

and I hadn't finished washing out the kitchen cupboards.

When I got home, we both worked hard for an hour. Only then did Mum allow us to stop for a coffee. To keep out of her way, I took boxes of stuff upstairs and put them in a corner. One was full of Mum's dancing trophies, which she won't put on display, no matter how much we nag her and keep on at ___line 46___ her to do so, but the other seemed to contain nothing but rubbish. Why were we carrying all this stuff from one place to another?

I sat down on the floor and began to sort through the junk. Perhaps I could get Mum to get rid of some of it? And then, as I dug into the box, my fingers met something luxuriously soft. Puzzled, I pulled it out and found myself holding a blue velvet drawstring bag with a squarish object inside. I turned it over in my hands, digging my fingernails into the dense, almost furry material. There was a line of embroidery around the top, a row of little suns and moons and stars, decorated with shiny sequins. I told myself sensibly that it wouldn't hold anything exciting, just broken jewellery or dry make-up. But I was rejecting these thoughts even as I lined them up. I just knew that this carefully decorated bag must contain something special.

1 Why did the girl feel cheated?
  A She hadn't realised how lonely she would feel.
  B She didn't want to see anyone else.
  C She found the area less attractive than she had expected.
  D She now felt obliged to go down to the bridge.

2 As the girl crossed the bridge, she wanted to give the impression that she
  A had only just noticed the boy there.
  B had made a sudden decision.
  C wasn't a very friendly person.
  D wouldn't let anything get in her way.

3 The girl was angry with herself in the third paragraph because she
  A was unable to go as fast as she wanted.
  B should have kept looking ahead.
  C was going in the wrong direction.
  D couldn't hold the boy's gaze.

4 How does the girl feel in the fourth paragraph after the incident with the boy?
  A disappointed that she had to go back to help her mother
  B upset with her parents for making her move
  C annoyed that it had changed her mood
  D irritated with herself for wasting so much time

5 What does 'as I did so' refer to in line 39?
  A leaned my head on my hands
  B feel sorry for myself
  C caught sight of my watch
  D jumped to my feet

6 What does 'nag her' mean in line 46?
  A congratulate her
  B complain about her
  C aim to inform her
  D try to persuade her

7 How does the girl react when she finds the bag?
  A She realises it is different from the other things she has come across.
  B She is certain her expectations of its contents will be disappointed.
  C She is immediately aware she should be careful when she opens it.
  D She thinks it probably isn't as old as it looks and feels.

8 Which of the following describes the girl?
  A She enjoys spending time on her own.
  B She tries to be positive when she has a problem.
  C She understands why people like collecting things.
  D She objects to people telling her what to do.

7 USE OF ENGLISH

Part 4

Grammar – Reported speech

Later in the evening the girl and her mother sat on the sofa together after cleaning the new house.

1 Read the conversation between the girl from the text on page 58 and her mother. Complete the reported speech in the text below.

How are you? You seem very quiet.

I'm feeling a bit sad because I've lived in Edinburgh all my life and now I'll have to make new friends. While you were shopping, I went for a walk and I saw a boy on the bridge. I wonder who he is.

Cheer up. Do you want to come shopping with me tomorrow to buy things we need for the house?

The girl's mum asked her how she (1) .... and said she (2) .... very quiet. The girl said to her that she (3) .... a bit sad because she (4) .... in Edinburgh all her life and now she (5) .... make new friends. She said that while her mum (6) .... shopping, she (7) .... for a walk and she (8) .... a boy on the bridge. She wondered who he (9) .... Her mum told her to (10) .... and asked if she (11) .... to go shopping with her the next day to buy things they (12) .... for the house.

2 Underline the verbs in the speech bubbles and those you have written. Complete this table.

Tense in direct speech	Tense in reported speech
present simple present continuous present perfect simple *will* past continuous past simple	past simple

3 Look at these two questions from Exercise 1. Write the reported sentences. When do we use *if* in the reported sentence?

How are you?

The girl's mum asked
....

Do you want to come shopping?

The girl's mum asked
....

4 Now report these questions.

1 Why are you so late?
   The teacher asked the boy ....
   ....

2 What are you watching?
   The girl's father asked her ....
   ....

3 Did you score a goal?
   The woman asked the boy ....
   ....

4 Is there any food left?
   The girl asked her mother ....
   ....

5 When will you be home?
   The boy's mother asked him ....
   ....

6 Have you seen my bag?
   The boy asked his sister ....

5 Which of these verbs fit into the gap in the sentence below? Which ones don't fit? Why?

> advised agreed asked encouraged explained mentioned persuaded reminded said told warned

The girl's mum .... her to clean the kitchen.

6 Now choose the correct verb in these sentences.

1 The teacher *reminded / explained* the children to bring the money for the trip.
2 We all *agreed / advised* to meet in the park that afternoon.
3 The weather forecast *told / warned* that it might snow.
4 You didn't *mention / remind* that Fiona was coming too.

7 ⊙ Exam candidates often make mistakes with reported speech. Choose the correct verb in these sentences.

1 They *told / said* that the weekend would cost £100 but that's not true because the weekend cost only £60 including lunch.
2 Anna *told / said* her friend that there was nothing to be afraid of.
3 In your letter you *told / asked* me if there was anything to see around Lake Frène.
4 Angela *told / said* her cousin not to wait for her.
5 So, the next day Pat went and *told / told to* his sister Mary that her friends were organising a surprise party for her birthday.
6 I *asked / said* my friend to wait for me.
7 Finally, I gave them the address and *told them / told* who I was.
8 When I *asked / asked to* my parents for permission, the answer was clear.

Ⓖ *See page 84*

Exam task

For questions 1–8, complete the second sentence so that it has a similar meaning to the first sentence, using the word given. Do not change the word given. You must use between two and five words, including the word given.

Example

I stopped learning to play the drums because the neighbours complained.
GAVE
The neighbours complained about the drums ....*so I gave up*........ learning to play them.

1 When I dropped my purse, a kind woman picked it up and ran after me.
BY
When I dropped my purse, ... a kind woman who ran after me.

2 'Don't leave your wet towel on the floor, Petra,' said her mum.
TOLD
Petra's mum .... leave her wet towel on the floor.

3 The teacher asked if anyone knew the age of the building.
HOW
The teacher said: '................................ old the building is?'

4 The film went on so long that they missed the bus home.
SUCH
It was .... that they missed the bus home.

5 My uncle said he didn't know why the computer wasn't working.
WHAT
My uncle said, 'I .... wrong with the computer.'

6 I didn't let my brother borrow my new football yesterday because he lost the last one.
LENT
I .... my brother my new football if he hadn't lost the last one.

7 The children can't wait to see their cousins again.
LOOKING
The children are .... their cousins again.

8 Jack said he would like to take up the guitar.
INTERESTED
Jack said he .... up the guitar.

> **Exam tip**
> Never leave an answer blank as each question is worth two marks in Use of English Part 4. ✓

Keeping up to date
READING · Science

3 Which science subject(s) do you like best? Why is it important to study science? Why do you think some people don't like studying science?

Exam task

You are going to read an article about some young scientists who entered a competition. For questions 1-15, choose from the people (A–D). The people may be chosen more than once.

> **Exam tip**
>
> Don't choose your answer just because a text mentions something similar to the question, e.g. more than one person talks about 'the survival of the planet' here (Q5) but only one mentions a responsibility.

Part 3

1 The students in the photos are studying different scientific subjects. Match each photo with one of the scientific areas in the chart. What are the students doing in the photos?

Photo		Photo		Photo ....
ecology	biology	chemistry	physics	mathematics
conservation	the human body	acids	atoms	algebra

2 Put these topics from a science course in the correct column. Are you studying any of these topics at the moment? Which ones?

~~acids~~ ~~algebra~~ ~~atoms~~ ~~the human body~~
cells ~~conservation~~ diseases ecosystems
electricity endangered species fractions
gases geometry genetics heat light
plastics mirrors percentages plants
pollution recycling robots sound

Which person

suggests taking a break and coming back to an idea?	1
recommends asking people to help come up with ideas for a project?	2
advises against changing an idea once work has started on it?	3
says presenting information in a variety of ways makes it accessible to more people?	4
feels a responsibility for the survival of the planet?	5
advises that a project should be achievable in terms of its aims?	6
says original ideas are likely to be more successful in the competition?	7
says the amount of effort required to get ready for the competition was challenging?	8
mentions the importance of a final technical check?	9
says being able to communicate ideas is more valuable than a vast amount of knowledge?	10
mentions that research of the topic should be as extensive as possible?	11
says taking part in the competition has increased their confidence?	12
suggests getting honest reactions about your work before the competition?	13
realises that it is impossible to absorb all the information they would like to?	14
suggests a way of researching presentation techniques?	15

Young Scientist Award

Four finalists from the Young Scientist Award competition talk about making a video and giving presentations to the judges.

A Maria *investigated the effects of energy drinks and produced one herself.*

Judges look for kids who are really excited about science. You might get inspired by topics which other kids have covered in the past and go on from that. But the judges are really looking for someone who has imagination. If you can make the judges think, 'Wow, I didn't think of that!', you're off to a good start. If you're having an idea-block, wait a day or two and look at it with fresh eyes. You'll find inspiration somewhere. Make sure that you have enough time to complete your video! Waiting until the last minute, when you are all rushed and stressed, isn't a good idea. If you have a plan laid out before you start anything, it helps keep you on track. Don't submit your video until you've got some feedback. Ask those friends whose opinions you can trust what they really think.

B Erik *invented a substance which can be painted on football boots to stop them attracting mud.*

I mixed with students from all over the country during the competition and we had some fun. There is a lot of media interest and talking to a reporter really brings you out of your shell. I'm less self-conscious now in adult company. The preparation before the day puts your commitment and determination to the test but it's more than worthwhile!! I think the best ideas come from everyday life – because that's where they are going to be put to use after all! Start brainstorming with your family and friends and write down every possibility which comes into your head. But make sure your project is realistic – it's pointless thinking you can stop global warming, for instance, as you don't have that much time or resources.

C David *has found a way of calculating how long bicycle tyres will last.*

I just want to know how everything in the universe works and survives, even though all that information would probably make my brain explode. I knew loads of smart kids would enter so I didn't think I had a chance at first. I took the opportunity because I thought it would be fun. For your video, pick a concept that you can explain so that it's visual and interesting. People have different learning styles so use different approaches to explain the same concept. Be enthusiastic about your topic and your viewers will be enthusiastic, too. There were definitely some finalists who had memorised a lot more science facts than me, but I was able to take a scientific concept and explain it in a simple way – in front of judges, television cameras and an audience. Good luck!

D Anita *produced lights which come on and go off automatically and can be attached to a bicycle or scooter.*

In the future I'd like to become an engineer and design sustainable technology. It is important for us to understand that we are the generation that must look after our precious resources on Earth. Entering this competition was a great experience for me. It's easy to feel unsure about your idea, get discouraged and think you should come up with something better, but stick with it. It's best if you know your topic backwards and forwards before you even begin to make the video. A brilliant video, which gets all the ideas across, isn't as easy as it looks so it's good to look at past entries from finalists and learn what factors contributed to make it one of the best. One of the hardest parts is fitting your information in two minutes. It seems like plenty of time, but it goes by so quickly! There's nothing worse than getting everything ready, and then finding out that a basic component of the video is wrong. So even if you think it's fine, play it through one last time.

Exam tip

The reading paper is one hour. Try to do each of Parts 1, 2 and 3 in 15 minutes, allowing five minutes for checking each one. Never spend more than 20 minutes on one part of the paper.

8 WRITING

Part 2: Essay

Grammar – Relative clauses

1 Complete these sentences from the texts on page 63 with the correct relative pronoun (*who*, *which*, *when*, *whose*). Go back to the text if you need to.

Defining clauses

1 But the judges are really looking for someone .... has imagination.
2 Write down every possibility .... comes into your head.
3 You might get inspired by topics .... other kids have covered in the past.
4 Ask those friends .... opinions you can trust what they really think.

Non-defining clauses

5 A brilliant video, ... gets all the ideas across, isn't as easy as it looks ...
6 Waiting until the last minute, ... you are all rushed and stressed, isn't a good idea.

2 Now answer these questions.

1 In which sentence could you omit the relative pronoun? Why?
2 In which sentences could you put *that* instead of *who* or *which*?
3 What is the difference in punctuation between defining and non-defining clauses?

3 Read the first two paragraphs of a candidate's essay. Complete the text with relative pronouns, indicating where *that* or no pronoun are possible alternatives.

> All students should study science until they are at least 18. Do you agree?
>
> I certainly agree that all students should study science at school. It's a subject (1) .... is incredibly important in our world today. However, I think the issue of how long students should study it is more difficult. If you are the kind of student (2) .... main interest is to become a doctor or a physicist, then certainly you will want to study science until you are 18. You will probably enjoy it too, because science is the subject (3) .... you
>
> are interested in, and probably the one (4) .... you are good at.
>   But less able students, (5) .... find it difficult to pass exams in physics, biology and chemistry, will not be enthusiastic. These subjects, (6) .... can be hard at higher levels, sometimes prove too challenging for them. The students then get very frustrated with science, (7) .... means they will behave badly in class as a result. That will make things very difficult for the teachers (8) .... are responsible for them.

4 Read these two possible conclusions to the essay. Are they both suitable? Why? / Why not?

> A Therefore, I would like to conclude by saying that for the reasons I have given above, all students should study science until they are 18. It will be an advantage for every country to have students who are well trained in science.

> B In my country, students study science until they are 16, and then choose whatever subjects they like until they are 18. I think this is a good system. I would like to conclude by saying that I do not agree that all students should study science until the age of 18.

5 It is important to plan an essay before you start writing. With your partner, complete the plan for the essay below.

Paragraph 1:   good for everyone to study science (important subject)
                       good to study till 18 if ...
Paragraph 2:

6 These phrases can begin or end an essay. Mark them B or E.

1 I would like to conclude by saying that ...
2 To start my discussion of this question, I would say that ...
3 The first thing I would like to say is ...
4 To conclude, I would say that ...
5 I will close by saying that I understand both points of view ...
6 My first reaction to this question is that ...

G *See page 85*

7 Choose the correct verbs in this essay. Use a dictionary if you need to.

<u>Some people say it is too late to do anything about the problem of global warming. What do you think?</u>
Scientists (1) *discovered / identified* some years ago that our planet was getting warmer. They (2) *reveal / argue* that humans have caused this problem, because we are using up all our resources like water, and polluting the Earth with our cars and factories. They (3) *claim / conclude* that the atmosphere is now much thinner, and that the sun is now making our planet warmer each year. They have (4) *believed / warned* us that there will be major problems as a result of this global warming. In fact, most scientists would (5) *say / report* that the problems are already with us and some people (6) *think / express* that it is too late for us to do anything about it. We have floods, fires, drought and hunger in poor countries, terrible pollution in rich countries; there is nothing we can do.

I (7) *disagree / agree* very strongly with this idea. We cannot let our world be destroyed, we must save it for ourselves and our children. In every country governments are working to deal with pollution and to (8) *encourage / suggest* us all to live in a much greener way. Like many young people, I am optimistic. I am sure that we will find a way to deal with global warming and to save our planet. We have to.

> **Exam tip**
> You can improve the mark for your essay by using a range of vocabulary to express your ideas. ✓

8 Work in pairs. Discuss these questions.
1 How many paragraphs are there? What does each paragraph focus on?
2 What was the student's plan for this essay?
3 Do you think it is an effective answer to the question?
4 Are you optimistic or pessimistic about the problems caused by global warming? Why?

9 It's useful to use topic-specific vocabulary in your essay. Make a list of any vocabulary or phrases about global warming in the essay on the left that you could use in one of your own.

10 Look again at the essay about science (S) on page 64 and the one about the environment (E) on the left. Do they:

　　　　　　　　　　　　　　　　　　S　E

1 start with factual information?
2 start by agreeing with the statement?
3 give both sides of the argument?
4 finish with a personal view?

Exam task

Write an answer to one of the essay questions below. Write your answer in 120–180 words in an appropriate style.

1 You have had a discussion in your English class about the importance of studying certain subjects at school. Now your teacher has asked you to write an essay answering this question:

All students should study mathematics until they are at least 18. Do you agree?

Write your essay.

2 You have had a discussion in your English class about the part computers will play in the future. Now your teacher has asked you to write an essay answering this question:

Do you think in future it will be possible for robots to become doctors and teachers?

Write your essay.

- Remember your argument must be logical, so plan your essay carefully.
- Make sure you answer the question, and come to a clear conclusion.

 See page 91

USE OF ENGLISH Technology

Part 3

Vocabulary – Computers

1 Look at this spider diagram showing useful computer words. Complete the diagram with these words, then add some more that you use.

browser email log out spreadsheet update webcam

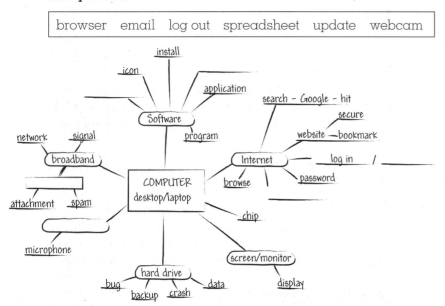

install
icon
application
Software
search – Google – hit
secure
network signal
website —bookmark
program
broadband
Internet
log in /
COMPUTER
browse
password
desktop/laptop
attachment spam
chip
microphone
screen/monitor
hard drive
bug
data
display
backup crash

2 Read these short texts about computers. Complete them with words from the diagram, in the correct form where necessary.

The Neptune is a powerful new laptop. With your purchase, we are offering an external hard (1) .... at a reduced price so you can automatically (2) .... up your files and store large amounts of (3) ....

You will be logged out of this website if there is no activity for more than ten minutes. Enter your **(4)** .... and email address to **(5)** .... in again. Don't forget to **(6)** .... this site so you can find it again easily.

Software updates are ready to be **(7)** .... Close any open **(8)** .... and then restart your computer.

Vocabulary – Word building (3)

3 Find words in Exercises 1 and 2 which are formed from the words below plus a suffix.

apply attach automatic easy power

Now complete the table below with words formed by adding one or two of these prefixes/suffixes.

-d dis- -(i)al en- -(il)ity -(it)ion -(it)ive -(it)or -ly un-

Verb	Noun	Adjective	Adverb
disable	....	ABLE	ably
....	....	....	....
		....	
	COMMERCE	....	....
		....	
COMPETE	....	....	....
	....	....	....

4 Which of these suffixes are always added to make nouns and which to make adjectives?

-d -al -ity -tion -ive -or

To make nouns, add: ....
To make adjectives, add: ....

> **Exam tip**
>
> In Use of English Part 3 there is always one word which has to be changed by adding a prefix (and sometimes a suffix too!).

5 Read this text to get a general understanding of what it is about. Some words are missing. For each gap decide if you need a noun, adjective or adverb.

Laptop computers

Portable computers first became
(1) .... available in 1981 but they were about the size of a sewing machine. Although they marked the beginning of **(2)** .... advances in the computer industry, they lacked the **(3)** .... to work on a battery so they never really gained in **(4)** .... Fortunately, work continued to reduce their **(5)** .... and size but it took another ten years of **(6)** .... in the computer industry. The older models were **(7)** .... too heavy and big to be on your lap but the name laptop became widely used. They are also known as notebooks. The laptop of today is **(8)** .... next to those earlier models but is now in **(9)** .... with smartphones and tablets which have become very **(10)** .... and do almost anything you might want!

---

6 Now use one or two of the prefixes/suffixes to change the words below so that they fit the gaps in the text in Exercise 5. (You do not need to use all the prefixes/suffixes.)

-able	-d	dis-	-ful	-al	-ly	-ity
-ion	-ive	-or	-ment	-t	un-	

1 commerce   *commercially*
2 technology   ....
3 able   ....
4 popular   ....
5 weigh   ....
6 develop   ....
7 actual   ....
8 recognise   ....
9 compete   ....
10 power   ....

7 Look back at the words in the gaps. Which one of them contains a prefix? Can you make any of the others negative by adding the prefix *un-* or *in-*?

8 Now make these words negative. Use one of the prefixes *dis-*, *im-*, *il-*, *in-*, *ir-*, *mis-* or *un-*.

---

approval experienced fortunate honesty legal patient
polite reliable responsible satisfied understanding

Exam task

For questions 1–10, read the text below. Use the word given in capitals at the end of some of the lines to form a word that fits in the gap in the same line. There is an example at the beginning (0).

> **Exam tip**
>
> Read the text through before you begin, and read it again when you have finished, to be sure it makes sense with the new words you have written. ✓

A SAILING BIKE

A teenager called Ned Aufenast has come up with
an **(0)** ....*impressive*........ way of getting about. It is   IMPRESS
a bicycle with a sail and it's quite a **(1)** ....   DRAMA
sight as Ned rides it through the traffic near his
home. **(2)** ...., he wasn't sure if he should   INITIAL
ride it on the road but, once he had given it
independent brakes, lights and reflectors, he was
given **(3)** .... to ride it anywhere except   PERMIT
on the motorways, where he would be doing so
(4) ....   LEGAL
Ned says his **(5)** .... came one day when he   INSPIRE
was riding his bicycle. It was a real struggle because
of the **(6)** .... of the wind. He's always been   STRONG
(7) .... about sailing and thought it might be   PASSION
fun to use wind power on the road. He says: 'You just
pedal and the wind helps you to go faster.' Although
not essential, his **(8)** .... of sailing was very   KNOW
(9) .... when he was designing the bike. A   HELP
Dutch company had already started **(10)** ....   PRODUCE
of something similar called the 'whike'. Ned is helping
them make versions based on his own design.

8 SPEAKING

Part 3

1 Work in pairs. Choose one of the pictures each and think about your answer to these questions.

Is this invention important to you?
Is it more or less important to other people in your family?
Do you use it every day or less often?

Tell your partner how important your chosen object is. Remember to give reasons.

2 🔘 1.21 Listen to two students discussing the seven objects in the photos. They are answering this question.

> • How important are these inventions in our daily lives?

1 Do they take turns to talk?
2 Do they ask each other's opinions?
3 Do they always agree?
4 Do they talk about each picture?

3 🔘 1.21 Listen again and write down what they say:

1 to start the conversation.
2 when they move to the next picture.
3 to ask each other's opinions.
4 when they agree with each other.

> **Exam tip**
>
> Don't spend too long on one photo. You only have three minutes for the whole conversation. Learn phrases you can use to move the conversation forwards. See Units 4 and 6. ✓

4 How many words/phrases can you think of that mean the same as *important*? Write them down.

5 🔘 1.21 It is better not to use the same word too many times. Listen again and add the words/phrases they use (for *important*) to your list. Did you already have some of them on your list?

6 🔘 1.22 Now listen to them discussing the second part of the question.

> • Which two do you think will become less important in the future?

What do they decide? Does it matter if they don't agree?

7 🔘 1.22 Listen again and write down what they say.

1 How do they move on to the second question? What does Karolina say?
2 What does Miguel say when he asks Karolina's opinion?
3 What does Miguel say about the bicycle to show he hasn't changed his mind?

Exam task

Work in pairs. Talk about the pictures together and answer both the questions.

> • How important are these inventions in our daily lives?
> • Which two do you think will become more important in the future?

Time your discussion. If it is too short, think of other things you can say.

Part 4

Exam task

Discuss these questions with a partner.

> • How important is technology at school? Which subjects is it essential for?
> • What do you use a computer for?
> • Do you enjoy watching TV? What programmes do you like?
> • Do you think technology stops people from talking to each other?
> • Do you think people are too dependent on mobile phones?
> • Some people say young children shouldn't watch TV. Do you agree?

> **Exam tip**
>
> When you answer a question, think about why, when or how. Always extend your answer. ✓

8 LISTENING

> **Exam tip**
>
> When you first see the question and possible answers, try to identify what the situation is and what you are being asked to do. It will help you to choose the correct answer. ✓

1 Work in pairs. Quickly read the eight questions below and match the situations with A–H.

A explaining an intention .....
B expressing feelings about something .....
C identifying a problem .....
D identifying travel details .....

E describing the weather for an event .....
F giving an opinion about something .....
G suggesting an activity others would like .....
H giving a purpose for speaking .....

Exam task

🎧 **1.23** You will hear people talking in eight different situations. For questions 1–8, choose the best answer, A, B or C.

1 You hear a brother and sister talking.
   What happened to the boy's work?
   A He lost it when the laptop crashed.
   B He saved it in the wrong place.
   C He forgot to save it.

2 You hear a sports programme on the radio.
   What will conditions be like for the race?
   A clear and sunny
   B wet and muddy
   C cold and icy

3 You hear a teacher talking to his class.
   Why is he talking to them?
   A to make a request
   B to pass on a complaint
   C to give instructions

4 You hear a boy and girl talking about school.
   What does the girl think of her maths lessons?
   A They're not well taught.
   B They're not very challenging.
   C They're not practical enough for her.

5 You hear a boy talking to his sister about a shopping trip.
   What does the boy say about the shopping trip?
   A He regretted playing a trick on his friends.
   B He was worried about losing his friends.
   C He and his friends disliked the crowds.

6 You will hear a girl talking to her class about her visit to an aquarium.
   What part of the visit does she recommend?
   A walking through the glass tunnels
   B handling some very unusual fish
   C seeing a marine art exhibition

7 You hear a boy talking about a cookery competition he entered.
   What is he aiming to do?
   A complain about what went wrong with a recipe
   B give instructions on how to make a difficult recipe
   C explain why he chose a particular recipe

8 You will hear a father and daughter talking about a holiday.
   How will the family get to the holiday centre?
   A by train
   B by car
   C by coach

REVISION

1 Choose the correct answer.

1 Don't forget to text me when you *arrive / will arrive*.

2 This is a great place to stay. We *camp / are camping* in a farmer's field.

3 Sorry, I *am not understanding / don't understand* what you're saying.

4 This time next week we *will sit / will be sitting* on the beach in the sun.

5 Paul says he knows that man but I *don't recognise / am not recognising* him.

6 I'll ring you back – I can't talk to you now because I *do / 'm doing* my homework.

7 Let me know as soon as you *hear / will hear* from Kamilla.

8 Children who *come / are coming* from large families get used to sharing their things.

2 Complete the second sentence so that it has a similar meaning to the first sentence, using the word given. Do not change the word given. You must use between two and five words, including the word given.

1 Usually, a modern city has wider streets than a historic city.
   AS
   Usually, the streets in a historic city .... those in a modern city.

2 Industrial areas tend to be very noisy compared to rural areas.
   FAR
   There is usually .... in industrial areas than in rural areas.

3 It takes my brother two hours to get to work but our father has a two-minute walk.
   MUCH
   My brother's journey to work .... our father's.

4 My favourite café is near the market square.
   BEST
   The café which I .... from the market square.

5 My friends and I don't go to the cinema as often as our parents do.
   LESS
   My friends and I go to the cinema .... our parents do.

3 Decide which word (A, B, C or D) best fits each gap.

1 There was a .... of opinion in my family about where to go on holiday, so in the end we stayed at home.
   A variation   **B** contrast   **C** difference   **D** disagreement

2 We found a quiet .... to have a picnic.
   A point   **B** spot   **C** situation   **D** site

3 My dad is going to make a .... decision tonight about whether I can go on the trip.
   A last   **B** latest   **C** finishing   **D** final

4 If you go on a cycle ride, you will get lots of .... air.
   A fresh   **B** pure   **C** clean   **D** natural

5 Peter wears strange clothes to .... attention to himself.
   A pull   **B** draw   **C** focus   **D** catch

6 If you want to be good at basketball, you will need to .... an effort to practise.
   A do   **B** give   **C** make   **D** take

7 When Fiona realised her secret had been discovered, she knew she was in serious ....
   A trouble   **B** problem   **C** fault   **D** concern

8 I .... my breath for ages so I could swim underwater.
   A kept   **B** cut   **C** stopped   **D** held

4 Complete this email from a student to her teacher with these phrases.

As for other ideas	I'm absolutely sure
I'm afraid that	I'm sorry to	We could
What about	What a great idea	Why don't we

Dear Mrs Wilson

Thanks for the email. (1) .... to have a barbecue for the whole class at the end of term. (2) .... everyone will think so. (3) .... asking Gabrielle if we can have it in her garden? Her family have a little swimming pool so we could swim too.

(4) .... invite her brother and sister to join us. We had a class barbecue there once before. (5) .... , there are lots of things we could do afterwards like going down to the beach or to the park.

(6) .... say I'm not very good at cooking but I'm sure some of the others are. I can bring some drinks and biscuits though.

(7) .... ask Alex and Tom to do the barbecue? They were really good at it last time.

(8) .... it might be difficult to find a day everyone can manage so we should start asking them now. I will send everyone a message.

Best wishes

Louisa

5 Match the two halves of the sentences and put the verbs into the correct past tense.

1 I hurt my hand
2 We got to the party so late that
3 We've been best friends
4 I've been trying to download this game for hours
5 I rang your doorbell six times yesterday
6 I've been to the new leisure park several times
7 I was playing the computer game you gave me
8 When I first met you last year,

a but you .... (not answer) so I went away.
b but I .... (not manage) to do it yet.
c when you .... (phone) me.
d while I .... (play) tennis.
e I was sure I .... (see) you before somewhere.
f our friends .... (already go) home.
g but I .... (not eat) in the café there yet.
h since you .... (come) to this school.

6 Complete the text with the verbs from the box, in the correct tense.

| be be go have invite |
| know let sail set shine |

My brother (1) .... sailing every weekend with his friends. He always says, 'When you (2) .... a bit older you can come with me.' I (3) .... fourteen next summer so maybe he (4) .... me go with him then. My uncle loves sailing and has a boat too. Last weekend he (5) .... me to go out with him. I (6) .... (never) with him before so I was really pleased. When we (7) .... out, the sun (8) .... but after about half an hour it got very windy. I (9) .... sailing lessons since September so I (10) .... exactly what to do. My brother was really surprised when we got back and my uncle told him what a great sailor I am!

7 Complete the sentences with adverbs formed from the adjectives below.

| careful definite easy excited immediate |
| particular simple usual |

1 The children ran round and round .... while they waited for the show to begin.
2 Michael says he's .... coming with us to the pool tomorrow.
3 Jonnie has a real talent for languages – he learns them ....
4 Football practice was due to start in ten minutes so we had to get changed ....
5 I .... listen to music in bed while I'm going to sleep.
6 I explained as .... as I could but they still didn't understand.
7 I carried the birthday cake to the table very .... as I didn't want to drop it!
8 Emma was .... good at maths so the school entered her in a competition.

8 Complete the sentences with an adjective formed from one of the words in the box.

| adventure centre fury mystery |
| nature predict rely suit |

1 There was a knock at the door, but nobody was there when we opened it – it was very ....
2 Our neighbour is looking for someone .... to babysit who will come every week at the same time.
3 My parents like to go to the same place on holiday – they're not very ....
4 This film isn't .... for my little sister as she's only six.
5 It's .... to feel a bit worried when you do something for the first time.
6 My brother was .... when he realised I'd worn his jeans.
7 Dad always makes the same jokes when my friends come round – he's so ....
8 My school is very .... so it's near all the shops.

Units 3 and 4

1 Choose the correct linking words.

1 *Despite / While* she was an excellent singer, Joanna could not play any musical instruments.

2 *Although / However* I have always liked travelling, I really dislike flying.

3 *Even though / In spite of* he is very good at maths, Peter simply isn't interested in it.

4 *Although / While* Paul tried to get to the concert on time, he arrived late.

5 *However / In spite of* being a great fan of James Bond films, George did not enjoy the latest one.

6 *Even though / However* my little sister likes school, she's always happy when the weekend comes.

7 *However / Despite* enjoying drawing, I wouldn't want to take art classes.

8 *Although / In spite of* I dislike dogs, they've never frightened me.

2 Complete the sentences with a passive verb.

1 Our French teacher cancelled the test because a lot of students were absent.
Our French test .... because a lot of students were absent.

2 My parents are sending me to a secondary school nearby because they like it.
I .... to a secondary school nearby because my parents like it.

3 Everyone in my family has played the same piano.
The same piano .... everyone in my family.

4 My teacher had advised me not to choose anything too ambitious for my science project.
I .... not to choose anything too ambitious for my science project.

5 The chef will take the biscuits out of the oven in 20 minutes if they're ready.
The biscuits .... out of the oven in 20 minutes if they're ready.

6 My grandmother is making me a prom dress.
My prom dress .... by my grandmother.

7 I borrowed those books from the school library.
Those books .... from the school library.

8 The school is putting the silver cup I won in the 100 metres on a special shelf.
The silver cup I won in the 100 metres .... on a special shelf at my school.

3 Complete the sentences with a person who works in the film industry.

1 The s................ t................ usually checks the quality of the recording on a film.

2 A s................ normally performs action shots, so the star can avoid dangerous situations.

3 A m................ a................ always does an actor's face and hair before he or she goes on set.

4 A p................ is responsible for raising money to make a film.

5 A c................ films the scenes and goes on location if necessary.

6 The d................ guides and instructs the actors on how to perform a scene.

7 A c................ d................ creates the clothes the actors wear on set.

8 The s................ d................ designs the scenery for the film set.

4 Which type of film would usually feature the following?

1 a spaceship, time travel and lots of special effects
2 funny scenes that make you laugh
3 a complicated plot with twists and turns
4 interesting factual information
5 cowboys and horses
6 characters that are drawn
7 moving figures or animals rather than real people
8 really frightening scenes, ghosts and monsters
9 car chases and people running across roofs
10 an amusing love story

5 Answer these questions about music.

1 Can you name three musical instruments that have strings?
2 Can you name three wind instruments?
3 Can you name five different types of music?
4 A pop group can also be called a ....
5 The words of a song are called ....
6 The music of a song is called the ....
7 A recording with a number of tracks is called an ....
8 The people who really like a particular group are called ....

6 Choose the correct modal verb (A, B or C) to complete the sentences.

1 You .... always check your homework before you hand it in.
   A ought   **B** should   **C** have to

2 You .... go to the party if you promise to be home by 11.00.
   A can   **B** must   **C** should

3 You .... to complete all the work for your science projects by next Friday.
   A must   **B** will have   **C** can

4 You .... drink any of that milk – it's gone off.
   A don't have to   **B** needn't   **C** mustn't

5 You .... won the competition if you hadn't fallen over on the ice!
   A should have   **B** could have   **C** must have

6 You .... been training really hard to have done so well in the 100 metres.
   A must have   **B** ought to have   **C** could have

7 I .... leave the house at 5.30 a.m. yesterday because the school trip started at 6.00 a.m.
   A could   **B** should   **C** had to

8 You .... asked me what to do if you were unsure.
   A needn't have   **B** should have   **C** must have

7 Complete these sentences with a preposition in each gap.

1 My brother is much more successful than me, but I've never been jealous .... him at all.

2 When you go on a school trip, your teachers are responsible .... your safety.

3 When the school week starts, I like to talk .... my friends about what I did at the weekend.

4 I've always been interested .... painting, and I'd like to take some art lessons.

5 I don't know if I can spend a week in London; it depends .... the cost of the accommodation.

6 Some elderly people find things to complain............... all the time, but my grandmother never does.

7 Could you possibly help .... the end-of-term party?

8 I'm really excited .... going to the big international hockey match next week.

9 Everyone knows that cold winters with a lot of snow are typical .... Canada!

10 Will you think .... which foreign language you want to study next?

8 Complete each paragraph below with words from the box above it. Add *s* or *'s* if necessary. There is one extra word in each list.

defender   goalkeeper   penalty
pitch   referee   tackle

A football match is always played on a (1) .... , with a (2) .... making sure the players on both teams play fairly. On each team, it's the attackers' role to score goals and the (3) .... job to keep them out of the goal, with help from two or three (4) .... All the players try to (5) .... the opposition in order to get the ball.

court   net   opponent   point   serve   umpire

In a tennis match it is the (6) .... who keeps the score. The player who starts the match has to (7) .... the ball to his/her (8) .... Every time a (9) .... is played, the ball must go over the (10) ....

9 Complete the lists with the correct form of each word.

	adjective	noun
1	convenient	....
2	equal	....
3	....	generosity
4	independent	....
5	....	patience

	verb	noun
6	conclude	....
7	connect	....
8	....	division
9	expand	....
10	....	persuasion

1 Match the two halves of the conditional sentences and put the verbs into the correct tense.

1 I might have enjoyed the school concert more
2 If I hadn't learnt to play the guitar,
3 Unless you live a long way away,
4 Take some money with you
5 I'll help you with your project
6 She will be late for school again
7 Most children never get to see a giraffe
8 If I could change one thing about my school,
9 Peter said he would try to learn some Chinese
10 You'll feel terrible in the morning

a if they .... (start) teaching it at his school.
b as long as you .... (help) me with mine!
c unless they .... (go) to a zoo.
d it .... (be) the uniform.
e it .... (be) best to cycle to school.
f if you .... (not get) a good night's sleep.
g I .... (miss) doing something I'm good at.
h unless she .... (set) her alarm clock.
i if there .... (be) some singing in it.
j in case you .... (need) to buy some lunch.

2 Complete the text with the correct form of the words in brackets.

Education in Britain

In Britain, children move to a (1) ....
(SECOND) school at the age of 11. The vast
(2) .... (MAJOR) of students go to a state
school rather than a private one. There
is no (3) .... (EXAMINE) you have to
pass to get in, and this type of mixed
ability school is known as a (4) ....
(COMPREHEND) school. However, students
are divided into different groups according
to their (5) .... (ABLE), a system known
as streaming. The most able students go
into the top set, where the most (6) ....
(CHALLENGE) work is done. All the students
study a (7) .... (VARY) of subjects,
including English, maths and science,
and also have the (8) .... (POSSIBLE) of
doing sport, art and music as part of their
timetable. At the age of 16, students have
the (9) .... (CHOOSE) of which subjects to
continue for the next two years, and at 18,
those who want to go on to university put
in their (10) .... (APPLY).

3 Complete the text with *a*, *an* or *the*, or leave a gap if necessary.

The Climate of Cape Town, South Africa

Cape Town has (1) .... Mediterranean climate, with
(2) .... mild, wet winters, and (3) .... dry and very warm
summers. In winter, which lasts from (4) .... beginning of
June to (5) .... end of August, (6) .... cold weather comes
across from (7) .... Atlantic Ocean bringing (8) .... heavy
rain and strong winds. (9) .... winter months are cool,
with (10) .... minimum temperature of 7 °C (45 °F). Most
of (11) .... city's annual rainfall occurs in wintertime, but
rainfall amounts for (12) .... different suburbs can vary
dramatically.
Summer, which lasts from (13) .... November to March,
is warm and dry. Cape Town gets frequent strong winds
from (14) .... south-east, known locally as the *Cape
Doctor*, because they blow away (15) .... pollution and
clean (16) .... air in the city. However, Cape Town can be
uncomfortably hot when the *Berg Wind* blows for (17) ....
couple of weeks in February or early March.
(18) .... Cape Town's weather is in fact remarkably similar
to that of San Francisco in (19) .... USA, although it is
definitely warmer, with (20) .... average air temperature
of 19 °C (66 °F) versus San Francisco's 13 °C (55 °F).

4 ⊙ Correct the mistakes in these sentences written by exam candidates.

1　I've never seen so beautiful roses in a garden.
2　When the concert started, everything was such exciting that the time flew.
3　I have so good memories from there, and I'd like to share them with you.
4　The book was such a good that I couldn't put it down.
5　It was great to hold the party on such marvellous evening.
6　I've never eaten a such tasty risotto before.
7　I love clothes and fashion is such important to me.
8　We had so a good laugh last time we met.
9　I have never stayed in a hotel which was such beautiful like this.
10　I had never trained with a such perfect volleyball team before.

5 Complete these short expressions by writing a word from the box below.

1　air ....
2　electrical ....
3　email ....
4　fresh ....
5　local ....
6　plastic ....
7　ready ....
8　recycled ....
9　reduce ....
10　take ....

> attachment　bags　conditioning
> equipment　ingredients　meals
> paper　produce　a shower　waste

6 Now complete this text with the expressions from Exercise 5.

If you want to live in an environmentally friendly way, there are lots of simple, practical steps you can take in your everyday life.

First of all, get your family to understand that it's important to (1) .... at home by cutting your energy consumption whenever possible. For instance, you can (2) .... rather than a bath and always ensure that you turn off (3) .... when you have finished with it. Never leave the television or computer on standby! And if you use the computer a lot, use (4) .... for printing and if at all possible send your homework by (5) .... instead of using paper. In addition, you should try to keep use of (6) .... in the home and family car to a minimum, even when it's very hot.

Remember too that you don't need (7) .... to take your shopping home when you go to the supermarket; it's much better to take a basket or box with you. When you're shopping for food, look for (8) .... rather than food that has been transported from miles away. Finally, if your family commits to healthy eating and you always prepare meals with (9) .... , you can avoid the huge amounts of packaging used to wrap the (10) .... you can find on the chilled counter.

7 Make adjectives from the words below, then complete the sentences with them.

1　competition ....
2　cheer ....
3　communicate ....
4　create ....
5　decide ....
6　determine ....
7　energy ....
8　sympathy ....

1　When I came home feeling unwell, my mum was very .... towards me.
2　My sister hates to lose – she's so ....
3　I knew I had to be .... , so I chose the answer very rapidly.
4　My grandfather has never been very .... but last week he sent me a long letter.
5　My cousin is very .... and she has just started her own business designing jewellery.
6　I was absolutely .... to pass the exam, so I studied really hard.
7　My best friend is always .... and I've never once seen her in a bad mood.
8　My little brother is incredibly .... and runs about all day without getting tired.

8 Complete the sentences with these verbs below. Use each verb only once.

> can't imagine　dislike　have never been able
> is looking forward　suggested　would like
> would prefer　would rather

1　I .... cycle to school than catch the bus every morning.
2　Susie .... to studying another language next year.
3　I .... to go to university if I get good grades in my exams.
4　Alison .... living apart from her twin sister.
5　Tim .... to take up judo rather than play tennis.
6　Most students of my age .... having homework to do every night.
7　I .... to do maths without a calculator.
8　I .... leaving at about 6.00 so we could get to the concert on time.

1 Choose the correct answer in italics.

My family arranged (1) *to go / going* away at the weekend to my uncle's cottage in the mountains. It wasn't a long journey but I still managed (2) *to fall / falling* asleep on the way because it was so hot. My father hadn't intended (3) *to stop / stopping* but we took a break by a lake halfway up the mountain to cool down. Luckily, I had suggested (4) *to take / taking* our swimming things in case we felt like (5) *to swim / swimming* in the stream near the cottage. We enjoyed (6) *to relax / relaxing* by the water for an hour or two and then we carried on (7) *to drive / driving* up the mountain. When we arrived at the cottage my mother tried (8) *to find / finding* the key in her handbag but it wasn't there. She said she remembered (9) *to put / putting* it in, and she made us (10) *to go / go* through all the other bags. In the end, we had to give up (11) *to look / looking* because it was getting dark. We had to choose between sleeping on the grass or going home so we decided (12) *to go / going* home. At least we had a nice swim in the lake!

2 Complete the second sentence so that it has a similar meaning to the first sentence, using the word given. Do not change the word given. You must use between two and five words, including the word given.

1 James said, 'I can't play football because I'm looking after my brother.'
EXPLAINED
James .... play football because he was looking after his brother.

2 Alice said, 'OK, I'll help you with your maths homework.'
AGREED
Alice .... me with my maths homework.

3 My friend said he couldn't come with us to the cinema because he'd forgotten his money.
SO
My friend said, 'I've forgotten my money .... with you to the cinema.'

4 My uncle said, 'This is the best show I've seen for years.'
SUCH
My uncle said he .... good show for years.

5 Anna said, 'I like your new dress.'
TOLD
Anna .... my new dress.

6 Archie asked me, 'Do you know how to play chess?'
IF
Archie asked me .... how to play chess.

3 Complete the sentences with these verbs.

come   dress   get   get   go   have
keep   look   make   show   suit   try

1 I .... in the same way as my friends.
2 I know what styles .... me.
3 I look for clothes that .... me look different from other people.
4 I .... rid of my old clothes when I'm tired of them.
5 Dark colours really don't .... good on me.
6 I like to .... up with the latest fashions.
7 Some people like to .... off by wearing all the latest fashions.
8 As soon as clothes .... out of fashion, I stop wearing them.
9 Sometimes clothes .... back into fashion after a few years.
10 I like to .... things on before I buy them.
11 I .... different tastes from my friends.
12 My friends like to .... dressed up when they go out.

4 Complete the sentences with these adjectives.

curious   frustrated   guilty
optimistic   passionate   patient

1 Mario has always been .... about basketball and hopes to be a professional player.
2 I was .... because I was trying to buy a ticket for the festival and my laptop wouldn't work.
3 Karim was really good at photography so he was .... about winning the competition.
4 I was .... to know where Jack was going so I followed him.
5 Elena felt .... about not going out with her friends as she had promised, so she phoned them all up to apologise.
6 There was a really long queue but we just had to be .... and wait for our turn.

5 These adjectives also fit in some of the gaps. Which ones? Look at the grammar as well as the meaning.

ashamed .... confident ....
enthusiastic .... furious ....
interested .... irritated ....

6 Complete the text with *who*, *which*, *whose* or *where*. When you have finished, go back and add *that* or – (nothing) to those gaps where they are possible.

Edwin Hubble, (1) .... was born in 1889, was an American astronomer (2) .... work has made a huge impact on what we know about the stars today. There is a telescope, an asteroid and a moon crater (3) .... are all named after him. As a child, Hubble was someone (4) .... was both a bright student and an excellent athlete. He went to the University of Chicago, (5) .... he studied mathematics, astronomy and philosophy. He spent most of his working life in California, (6) .... he formulated Hubble's Law, (7) .... helped astronomers determine the age of the universe and prove that it was expanding. At the time, astronomers knew only about the Milky Way, a galaxy of stars and planets (8) .... the Earth is part of. But with Hubble's work it became clear that there were many more galaxies beyond the Milky Way.

7 Read these definitions, then complete the words they define with the correct consonants.

1 when paper, glass, etc. is put through a process so that it can be used again

__ E __ __ __ __ I __ __

2 an illness often caused by an infection   __ I __ E A __ E

3 adjective describing animals and plants which may soon disappear from the world because there are so few left

E __ __ A __ __ E __ E __

4 the smallest basic unit of a plant or animal   __ E __ __

5 the protection of nature   __ O __ __ E __ __ A __ I O __

6 the scientific study of genes which control the particular characteristics of a living thing   __ E __ E __ I __ __

7 the smallest unit that an element can be divided into   A __ O __

8 a type of energy that can produce light and heat and make machines work

E __ E __ __ __ __ I __ I __ __

8 Complete the sentences with the correct form of the word in capitals at the end of each sentence.

1 You need a lot of .... in your arms to row a boat very far. **STRONG**
2 The argument against smoking is a very .... one. **POWER**
3 Our school was .... much smaller than it is now. **ORIGINAL**
4 We couldn't decide what to do as there were so many .... to choose from. **POSSIBLE**
5 It's .... to leave the table before everyone's finished eating. **POLITE**
6 Not enough young people attend the town festival – we need to make it more .... to them. **ATTRACT**
7 There are too many .... on this channel – they break up the programmes. **COMMERCE**
8 I was told to go to the school at 8.00 a.m. for a meeting but there must have been a .... because nobody was there. **UNDERSTAND**

Unit 1

Present tenses

We use the present simple

1   to say when things happen if they take place regularly:
    *I **meet** my friends on Saturdays.*
2   to talk about permanent situations:
    *I **live** in a small flat.*
3   to state general truths:
    *Teenagers **sleep** more than adults.*

We use the present continuous

1   to talk about the present moment:
    *Go away – I'm **watching** TV.*
2   for a temporary action or event:
    *I'm **staying** with my granny for a couple of days.*
3   for repeated actions and events over a period of time:
    *I'm **learning** to play the guitar. (But not exactly at the present moment.)*
4   for changing or developing situations:
    *The world **is getting** warmer.*

State verbs

These are generally used in a simple tense (i.e. not a continuous tense). They are mostly about thoughts, feelings, belonging and the senses. Here are some common examples: *believe, know, mean, remember, suppose, understand, feel (= believe), think (= believe), adore, despise, hate, like, love, want, wish, prefer, belong, have/have got (= possess), own, smell, taste, hear, see, feel, contain, seem, look (= seem), weigh:*
> *I **like** our new flat.*
> *I **have** three sisters.*

Present tenses in future clauses

In clauses referring to future time and which begin with *when, until, before, after, as soon as,* we use the present simple:
> *I'll call you when I **get** to my friend's. (**not** ... ~~when I will get~~)*

or the present perfect:
> *I'll have dinner when I**'ve finished** my homework. (**not** ... ~~when I will have finished~~)*

The future

We use the present simple for scheduled events with a future meaning:
> *The bus **leaves** for London at 8.15 on Saturday.*

We use the present continuous for plans which are already arranged:
> *We**'re playing** football on Wednesday.*

We use *will*

1   for decisions made at the moment of speaking:
    *The phone's ringing. I**'ll answer** it.*
2   for anything which is uncertain, especially with *probably, maybe, I think, I hope* and *I expect*:
    *I probably **won't finish** this project today.*
3   for predictions (as they are not definite):
    *The number of people on the planet **will grow** to nine billion by 2050.*
4   for requests, promises, offers:
    *I**'ll give** you your book back on Friday.*

We use *going to*

1   for something we have decided to do but which isn't a definite arrangement: *I'm **going to ring** my friend in a minute.*
2   to predict something when we have some evidence:
    *It**'s going to rain**. (I can see the clouds.)*

We can often use either the present continuous or *going to* for plans:
> *I'm **meeting** / I'm **going to meet** my friends in town.*

We use the future continuous for an event happening at a particular time or over a period of time in the future:
> *I can't come at 6.00 as I**'ll be looking** after my sister.*

Comparisons

1 syllable (warm)	2 syllables ending in -y (happy)	2 or more syllables (expensive)
warmer (than)	happier (than)	more expensive (than)
(the) warmest	(the) happiest	(the) most expensive

Some two-syllable adjectives (e.g. *quiet, polite*) and adjectives ending in *-ow, -er* and *-le* can take both forms:
> *Jo is **more polite** than Sam. = Jo is **politer** than Sam.*

Irregular adjectives:
> *good, better, best*
> *bad, worse, worst*
> *far, farther/further, farthest/furthest*

We use comparative structures to compare people or things

1   with an adjective:
    *My brother is **taller than** my sister.*
    *My sister **isn't as tall as** my brother.*
    *I'm **as good** at football **as** my older brother.*
    *This TV programme is **less interesting than** last week's.*
2   with a noun: *I get **more/less pocket money than** you.*

Unit 2

Past tenses

We use the past simple for
1 completed actions and events in the past:
   *I **went** to the city centre yesterday.*
2 repeated actions and events in the past:
   *I **practised** the guitar every day before the concert.* (But the concert's over now so I don't practise every day.)
3 permanent or long-term situations in the past:
   *My family **lived** in Paris for four years.* (But they don't now.)

We use the present perfect simple
1 to talk about a period of time which is still continuing, sometimes with *since* or *for*:
   *I**'ve lived** in this village for five years.* (And I continue to live here.)
2 for unfinished actions and events, sometimes with *still* or *yet*:
   *I **haven't been** to the new pool yet.* (But I hope I will go there.)
3 for events that happened in the recent past, sometimes with *just*:
   *She**'s gone** to the cinema.* (And she's still there.)
4 to talk about how many times something has happened, sometimes with *already*:
   *I**'ve (already) heard** this band several times.*

We use the present perfect continuous (often with *since* or *for*) when we want to emphasise the activity rather than the result.
Compare:

   *I**'ve been reading** this book for weeks.* (I still haven't finished it.)
   *I**'ve read** four books this week.* (I've finished them.)

*I**'ve been doing** my homework while you've been out.* (That's how I spent the time.)

*I**'ve done** my homework while you've been out.* (I've finished it.)

We use the past continuous
1 to talk about a particular moment in the past:
   *I **was listening** to the radio at 8.30 this morning.*
2 for an activity beginning before a past action (usually in the past simple) and continuing until or after it:
   *I **was going** upstairs when I **heard** a strange noise.*
3 for two things happening at the same time:
   *It **was pouring** with rain while we **were playing** football.*

We use the past perfect simple
1 to refer to an earlier time when we are already talking about the past, often with time expressions like *when*, *after*, *by the time*, *as soon as*:
   *By the time I was six, I**'d lived** in three different places.*
2 with adverbs like *just*, *already*, *before*, *ever* and *never*:
   *Jasmine offered to lend me her book but I**'d** already **finished** my homework.*

We use *used to* and *would* to talk about past habits when we are emphasising they are no longer true. *Used to* is more common than *would*:
   *My mum **used to sing** to me every night.*
   *= My mum **would sing** to me every night.*
Used to can describe actions and states, but *would* can only describe actions:
   *My brother used to live in Sydney. **not** My brother ~~would live~~ …*

Adverb formation

Many adverbs are formed from adjectives by adding the suffix *-ly*, but note the following.
Adjectives ending in *-y* change their last letter to *-i* before adding *-ly*: *angry* → *angrily*
Adjectives ending in consonant + *-le* lose the last letter before adding *-ly*: *probable* → *probably*
Adjectives ending in *-e* keep the *-e* and add *-ly*: *rare* → *rarely*
Adjectives ending in *-l* double the *-l* before they add *-ly*: *careful* → *carefully*

The passive

Active	Passive
Kai **plays** lead guitar.	Lead guitar **is played** by Kai.
The DJ **is playing** my favourite song now.	My favourite song **is being played** by the DJ now.
The band first **recorded** the song in 2009.	This song **was** first **recorded** by the band in 2009.
Lots of different people **have sung** this song.	This song **has been sung** by lots of different people.
You **can download** the track for free.	The track **can be downloaded** for free.
The band's fans **will buy** their new album.	The new album **will be bought** by the band's fans.
The shops **had sold** a million copies of the album by midday.	A million copies of the album **had been sold** by midday.

The passive is used when
1 we don't know who or what does/did something:
   *My bike **was stolen** from outside the school.*
2 the action is more important than who does/did it:
   *The match **has been cancelled** because of the weather.*
3 it is obvious who or what does/did something:
   *The film **will be shot** in Brazil.*
We can use *by* + person/thing to show who does/did the action if this is important information:
*This song **was written** by Chris Martin.*

Verbs with two objects in the passive
There are two ways of making the passive of verbs that take two objects (e.g. *give, show, tell*):
*The boy band **was given** first prize.*
*First prize **was given** to the boy band.*

have something done
We use the structure *have* + thing/person + past participle when someone else does something for us:
*She **had** her hair and make-up **done** before going on the stage.*

Linking words and phrases

We use *in spite of, despite, although, even though, but, however* and *while* to contrast two ideas or events. *Despite* and *in spite of* are prepositions; they are followed by *-ing*, a noun or by *the fact that* + subject + verb:
*The singer finished the show **despite having** a sore throat.*
*They continued filming **despite the bad weather**.*
*The concert was a success **in spite of the fact that** the guitarist was new.*

Although and *even though* are conjunctions; they are followed by a noun/pronoun and a verb:
*They continued filming **although/even though** the weather was bad.*
*She never sings her own songs **although/even though** she's written a lot.*

But and *however* have the same meaning. *But* joins two halves of a sentence. *However* contrasts two separate sentences and is more formal than *but*:
*Johnny Depp is a really good actor **but** I didn't enjoy his latest film.*
*Johnny Depp is a really good actor. **However**, I didn't enjoy his latest film.*
*Johnny Depp is a really good actor. I didn't, **however**, enjoy his latest film.*

While can go at the beginning or in the middle of a sentence:
***While** I know he's a very good writer, I still don't like his books.*
*Annie has dark hair and eyes **while** her brother is the opposite.*

Modal verbs

Obligation

We can often use either *must* or *have to* with the same meaning:

> I **must / have to phone** my mum now.

We use *must* to give orders or strong advice, including to ourselves:

> I **must remember** to bring my football boots tomorrow.
>
> You **must try** harder.

When there is a rule or where the obligation does not come from the speaker, *must* is possible but *have to* is more usual:

> We **have to be** at football practice early tomorrow.

We normally use *have to* for habits:

> I **have to practise** every day.

We only use *must* in the present tense. In all other tenses, we use *have to*:

> I **had to buy** new football boots because my feet had grown.
>
> We**'ll have to find** a new goalkeeper because Matt is ill.

Although *must* and *have to* both express obligation, *mustn't* and *don't have to* have different meanings:

> You **mustn't wear** shoes in the gym. (Don't do it.)

We also say *You can't* or *You're not allowed to*.
We use *don't have to* when there is **no** obligation to do something:

> I **don't have to take** any money because the bus is free. (It's not necessary to do it.)

We can also say *You don't need to* or *You needn't*.

Permission and advice

We use *can* to mean 'it is possible' or 'it is allowed':

> You **can borrow** my tennis racket if you want.

When we are talking about the right thing to do, we use *should(n't)* or *ought (not) to*:

> You **should tell** your parents where you are going.

Expectations

When we expect something to happen, we use *should (not)*:

> Our team **should do** well today as we've practised so much.

We also use *should* when we discover a situation is not as we expected it:

> My phone **should be** in my pocket because that's where I left it.

In the past, we say *should(n't) have*:

> We **should have scored** more goals as we had lots of chances.

Ability

We use *can* or *be able to* to say someone has an ability:

> My brother **can** cook but he's very bad at washing up.

We use *could* or *was able to* to say someone had an ability:

> I **could speak** two languages when I was little.

In all other tenses, we use a form of *be able to* to talk about ability:

> I **won't be able to come** skiing because I've hurt my foot.

Certainty and possibility

In the present we use

1 *must* when we are sure something is true:
> Those boots **must belong** to Cameron. He's got big feet.

2 *can't/couldn't* when we are sure something is not true:
> That **can't be** Sara because she doesn't come to this school any more.

3 *might/may/could* when we think something is possible:
> This text **might be** from Dan but it doesn't say.

4 *might not/may not* when we think something is uncertain:
> I'll phone him but he **might not be** there.

Could means the same as *may/might* (something is possible) but *couldn't* means something is not true, which is different from *may not/might not* (something is uncertain).

In the past we use

1 *must have* when we are sure something is true:
> Claire's coat isn't here so she **must have gone** home.

2 *can't/couldn't have* when we are sure something is not true:
> Claire's coat is here so she **can't/couldn't have gone** home.

3 *might/may/could have* when we think something is possible:
> Adam **might have borrowed** my bike because it's not here and his is broken.
>
> Luca isn't here. He **might/may/could have forgotten** to come because we changed the day.

4 *might/may not have* when we think something is uncertain:
> You **might/may not have heard** Ellie's good news because you weren't here yesterday.

Could have means the same as *may/might have* (something is possible) but *couldn't have* means something is not true, which is different from *may/might not have* (something is uncertain).

Unit 5

Conditionals

- *If + present simple, + present simple*

We use the zero conditional to state general facts and truths:

> *Children* **do** *better at school* **if they sleep** *well.* (This is **a known fact**.)
> **If** *children* **sleep** *well, they* **do** *better at school.*

- *If + present simple, + will/modal + infinitive*

We use the first conditional for a future condition which we believe is possible or likely:

> **If** *you* **give** *me some money, I* **'ll buy** *a ticket for you.*
> **If** *you* **chat** *to your friends during lessons, you* **won't learn** *anything.*
> *I* **can** *cycle to school tomorrow* **if I feel** *better.* (I think I will feel better.)

- *If + past simple, + would/could + infinitive*

We use the second conditional for an imaginary condition which we believe to be impossible or unlikely. We use the past tense although the speaker is thinking about the present or the future:

> *You* **would win** *first prize if you* **practised** *more.*
> *I* **could reach** *that shelf if I* **were** *taller.* (But I'm not taller so I can't reach.)

! We can use *were* or *was* after *if I/he/she/it*.

Compare the first and second conditionals:

> **If** *you* **spent** *more time on your homework, you* **would get** *better marks.* (But you almost certainly won't spend more time.)
> **If** *you* **spend** *more time on your homework, you* **'ll get** *better marks.* (more likely)

- *If + past perfect, + would/could/might have + past participle*

We use the third conditional to talk about past events which cannot be changed, so we know the condition is impossible:

> **If** *my dad* **hadn't driven** *me to school, I* **would have been** *late.* (But he drove me so I wasn't late.)
> *My friend* **would have been** *upset if I* **'d forgotten** *her birthday.* (But she wasn't upset because I didn't forget.)

We sometimes see sentences which contain a mixture of second and third conditionals because of their context:

> *I* **wouldn't have lost** *my purse* **if** *I* **were** *more careful.*
> (I did lose it because I am generally not very careful.)

Compare: *I* **wouldn't have lost** *my purse* **if** *I* **had been** *more careful.* (On this particular occasion I wasn't careful.)

We can start conditional sentences with either the *if*-clause or the main clause. If we put the main clause first, there is no comma between the clauses:

> *If you smiled more, you'd make friends.*
> *You'd make friends if you smiled more.*

Other ways of expressing *if*

Unless, in case, as/so long as, provided (that) / providing (that)

All these expressions are followed by the present tense even when we are talking about the future.

1. *Unless* means 'except if':
   > *You'll get a ticket if you get in the queue early.* =
   > *You won't get a ticket* **unless** *you get in the queue early.*

2. We use *in case* when we do something because something else might happen:
   > *I'll tidy my room* **in case** *my friends want to go in there.* (I'll tidy it now before they come because they might want to go in there.)
   > *In case* doesn't have the same meaning as *if*:
   > *I'll tidy my room* **if** *my friends want to go in there.* (I won't tidy it before they come because they might not want to go in there.)

3. *As/so long as* and *provided (that) / providing (that)* can be used instead of *if* and mean 'only if' or 'on the condition that':
   > *I'll go to the party* **as/so long as** *you come too.*

I wish

To say we would like a present situation to be different, we use *I wish / If only + past simple*:

> *I wish* **I had** *my own bedroom.* (But I don't.)

To say we want something to happen or someone (not) to do something, we use *I wish / If only + would + infinitive*:

> *If only the rain* **would stop**.

> *I wish my mum* **would let** *me stay up later.*

To express a wish or regret about the past we use *I wish / If only + past perfect* (it's like a third conditional):

> *My mum wishes she* **hadn't bought** *this car.* (Because it goes wrong all the time.)

Unit 6

Countable and uncountable nouns

Nouns can be either countable, e.g. *bed, child, trip,* or uncountable, e.g. *accommodation, advice, experience, homework, information, music, news, pollution.*
Some nouns can be both but with different meanings:

*These maths **exercises** are easy.* [C]
***Exercise** is good for you.* [U]

Countable nouns

1 can be singular and have *a/an* before them: *a cat, a job, an adventure*
2 can be plural (sometimes with *many/few/some* or a number before them): *some friends, many animals, three buses*

Uncountable nouns

1 cannot be plural: *Take my advice* (**not** ~~advices~~)
2 take a singular verb: *This food is delicious.*
3 can have *some/much/little* before them: *some bread, not much information, a little homework.*
4 can use other words to refer to quantity: *a slice of bread, a piece of paper*

Articles

A(n), the and no article

A(n) is used with singular countable nouns and introduces a new item of information:

*I have **an** idea.*

The is used with countable and uncountable nouns, for items mentioned before or when the speaker and listener both know what they are talking about:

*There's **a** mouse in **the** kitchen.* (The mouse is new but the speaker and listener know which kitchen.)

We don't use an article with plural countable and uncountable nouns when we talk about things in a general sense. Compare:

***Musicians** don't earn much.* (musicians in general)
***Music** makes people feel better.* (music in general)
***The music** is too loud.* (this particular music which is playing now)

Special uses of articles

The is used with

- oceans, seas and rivers (*the Black Sea, the Thames*).
- regions (*the south of France, the Far East*).
- groups of islands (*the Philippines*).
- names of countries that include a word like *republic, kingdom* or *states* (*the United States*).
- deserts and mountain ranges (*the Alps, the Kalahari Desert*).

We don't use *the* with

- lakes (*Lake Garda*).
- continents, most countries, states, cities, towns and villages (*Europe, Florida, Rome*).
- buildings and locations which use a name (*John Lennon Airport, Edinburgh University*).
- many common expressions: *by train/bus, at home, at work, in hospital, have lunch/dinner, watch television* (but *listen to the radio*).

So and such (a/an)

So and *such* mean 'as much as this'.
So is followed by

1 an adjective: *Global warming is **so worrying**. The giraffes were **so tall** that you could see them above the trees.*
2 an adverb: *The lion came **so close** (that) everyone was scared.*
3 *much, many* and *few* with or without a noun: *There were **so many people** (that) we couldn't see. I ate **so much** (that) I could hardly move.*

Such is followed by

1 *a/an* (+ adjective) + singular noun: *It was **such a good film** (that) I wanted to watch it again. I had **such a surprise** when the doorbell rang.*
2 (adjective +) plural noun: *There were **such problems** (that) we had to cancel the trip. I had **such good results** in the test (that) my parents gave me a laptop.*
3 (adjective +) uncountable noun: *The trip was **such fun**. This is **such strong glass** (that) it will never break.*
4 *a lot / a lot of* (+ noun): *There was **such a lot** to tell my mum (that) I didn't know where to start. My uncle has **such a lot of money** (that) he doesn't know what to spend it on.*

Too and enough

Enough means 'sufficient, the right quantity' and *too* means 'more than enough'. We use *too* and *enough* with adjectives, adverbs and nouns.
Enough goes

1 before a noun: *I've got **enough money**.*
2 after an adjective: *I'm not **old enough** to drive.*
3 after an adverb: *We didn't run **quickly enough**.*

Too goes

1 before *much/many* + a noun: *I've got **too much homework**.*
2 before an adjective: *I'm **too young** to drive.*
3 before an adverb: *He ran **too quickly** for us to catch him.*

Verbs and expressions followed by *to*-infinitive or *-ing* form

- Verb + *to* + infinitive, e.g. *(can't) afford, agree, aim, appear, arrange, attempt, decide, demand, deserve, fail, forget, hope, learn, manage, offer, plan, pretend, refuse, seem, tend, (can't) wait*:

  You **deserve to do** well.
  She **pretended not to notice**.

- Verb (+ <u>object</u>) + *to* + infinitive, e.g. *ask, choose, expect, help, intend, prepare, promise, want*:

  We **expect to arrive** by 6.00.
  We **expected** <u>them</u> **to wait** for us.

- Verb + <u>object</u> + *to* + infinitive, e.g. *dare, encourage, force, invite, order, persuade, remind, teach, tell, warn*:

  My friend **dared** <u>me</u> **to jump** across the river.

- *Make* and *let* are followed by the infinitive without *to* and always have an object:

  I **made** <u>my brother</u> **come** shopping with me.

- Verbs followed by *-ing* form, e.g. *avoid, can't help, can't stand, carry on, consider, delay, dislike, enjoy, feel like, finish, give up, imagine, involve, keep/keep on, mention, (not) mind, miss, postpone, practise, put off, suggest*:

  I **suggested playing** badminton instead of tennis.
  I **enjoy not having** much to do on Sundays.

- Verbs and expressions ending in a preposition always take *-ing*:

  I **gave up doing** gymnastics when I hurt my foot.
  I am **interested in becoming** a fashion designer.

- Some verbs are followed by either the *to*-infinitive or *-ing* form with little or no difference in meaning, e.g. *begin, can't bear, continue, hate, like, love, prefer, propose, start*:

  I **prefer to shop** / I **prefer shopping** at the market.
  ! *would like*, *would prefer* and *would love* are always followed by the *to*-infinitive.

- Some verbs can be followed by the *to*-infinitive or *-ing* but with a difference in meaning, e.g. *remember, forget, mean, go on, try, stop*:

  Remember to take your keys with you. (something you have to do)
  I **remember taking** my keys with me. (a memory of a past action)
  Try to walk faster. (Attempt to do it if you can.)
  Try taking more exercise. (a suggestion or experiment)

Reported speech

Tenses

When we report what someone said (direct speech, e.g. *I am cold*), we are usually reporting some time after the actual speech so we change the tenses used by the speaker (reported speech, e.g. *He said he was cold.*).

direct speech	→	reported speech
present simple	→	past simple
present continuous	→	past continuous
will	→	would
is/am/are going to	→	was/were going to
present perfect	→	past perfect
past simple	→	past perfect
past continuous	→	past perfect continuous
can/may	→	could/might

If the verb in direct speech is past perfect, we don't change it. These verbs don't change either when they are reported: *could, would, might, ought to* and *used to*.

! When we report *must*, we usually use *had to*:

  '*I* **must buy** some new trainers.' → She said she **had to buy** some new trainers.

but we use *must not* had to when we report a negative or a deduction:

  '*You mustn't tell Sam.*' → She said we mustn't tell Sam.
  '*Giulia must be tired.*' → She said that Giulia must be tired.

Say and tell

We often use *say* and *tell* to report speech:

  He **said** (that) he would be late.
  He **said to me** (that) he would be late. (**not** *He said me ...*)
  He **told me** (that) he would be late. (**not** *He told to me ...* or *He told that ...*)

Other common reporting verbs are *add, agree, answer, explain* and *reply*. The *to*-infinitive is usually used after them: *He promised/agreed to be quiet.*

Reporting questions

When we report questions we don't use the question form of the verb and there is no question mark.

Questions with question words (*who, what, how*, etc.) keep the question words when reported:

  How do you feel? → Peter asked Tom how he felt. (**not** *Peter asked Tom how did he feel.*)

Questions we can answer with *yes* or *no* are reported with *if* or *whether*:

  '*Do you like my new shoes?*' → Rachel asked Tom **if**/**whether** he liked her new shoes.

Relative clauses

We use *which, who, where, when* or *whose* to join two ideas about a thing or things:

> *This is my camera. I had it for my birthday. It has stopped working.*
> → *This camera, **which** I had for my birthday, has stopped working.* (**not** ~~which I had it for my birthday~~ – We use *which* instead of *it*.)
> *The pool **where** we usually swim is closed today.*

There are two kinds of relative clause: defining and non-defining.

- Defining relative clauses tell us essential information about the things or people they refer to:
  The girl <u>who won the competition</u> lives next door to me. (If we remove the underlined words, we don't know which girl is being described.)
  The shop <u>where I bought this laptop</u> has a sale. (If we remove the underlined words, we don't know which shop.)
  The boy <u>whose father owns the garage</u> sold me his bicycle. (If we remove the underlined words, we don't know which boy.)

- Non-defining relative clauses tell us extra information about the things or people they refer to:
  My brother, <u>who is three years older than me</u>, won a competition yesterday.
  My bicycle, <u>which I haven't had very long</u>, is too small for me.
  (The important information is about the competition / size of the bicycle and the underlined words are extra information – we don't need them.)

Defining relative clauses

1 are never separated from the rest of the sentence by commas:
The bag which I left on the bus was never found.

2 often use *that* instead of *who* or *which*:
*Who is the girl **that** you were talking to?*
*There's a new shop in the village **that** sells computer games.*

3 often omit the relative pronoun if it is the object of the verb in the relative clause:
*The programme about famous scientists (**which/ that**) I saw last night was really interesting.*
(The relative clause begins with a new subject (*I*) so we can omit *which/that*.)
We can say:
The bus which/that I usually catch to school didn't come today. or
The bus I usually catch to school didn't come today.
but we keep the relative pronoun if it is the subject of the verb in the relative clause:
The scientist who was on TV last night works with my dad. (*was* refers back to the scientist so we can't omit *who*.)
~~The scientist was on TV last night works with my dad.~~

Non-defining relative clauses

1 must be separated from the rest of the sentence by commas:
Sam's granny, who lives in Switzerland, used to be a champion skier.

2 never use *that*:
My uncle, who is an actor, often comes to stay.
not ~~My uncle, that is an actor, often comes to stay.~~

3 never omit the relative pronoun:
*Katya, **whose** family own a restaurant, is coming to the film with us.*

4 sometimes refer to the whole of the main clause:
*My cousins in Canada have invited me to spend the summer with them, **which** is really fantastic!*
(The idea of spending the summer in Canada is fantastic.)

Prepositions in relative clauses

In informal sentences, we put the preposition at the end:
That's my sister. The teacher is talking to her.
→ *That's my sister **who** the teacher is talking **to**.*
Peter had a party. He invited me to it. It was very good.
→ *Peter's party, **which** he invited me **to**, was very good.*
If the sentence is very formal, we can put the preposition before the relative pronoun:
*We will address the problem **to which** you refer at the school council meeting.*

This guide will help you prepare for Writing, Paper 2 of Cambridge English: First for Schools. The practice tasks and model answers will help you to see what is expected and what makes a good answer to the writing tasks.

Planning and timing

There are two parts to the writing paper, which lasts one hour and 20 minutes.

Writing Part 1

- This is compulsory. You have to write 120–150 words.
- In Part 1 you are guided through the task by the instructions and notes.
- Allow five minutes for reading and planning, and 25–30 minutes for writing.

Writing Part 2

- This has a choice of four questions. You have to write one answer of 120–180 words.
- In Part 2 you have to choose your question, and then plan it yourself.
- Allow five minutes for choosing your question and planning it and 30 minutes for writing.

Leave ten minutes at the end of the exam for checking the grammar, spelling and punctuation of your work.

Writing Part 1

Email or letter

(See Units 1 and 4, pages 12 and 36.)

Planning

- Read the instructions, email or letter and make sure you understand the situation.
- Decide whether the writer of the email or letter is a friend, a stranger or someone else.
- Decide on your style (formal, semi-formal or informal).
- Look at the four prompts and make sure you understand what you have to write for each one.

Practice task and model answer

1 Read the instructions and the email and answer the questions.

1 Who is the email from and what is your relationship to the writer?
2 What is the email about?
3 Is the style formal/semi-formal/informal? Which phrases show this? Underline them.
4 Which style should you reply in?

Your class wants to hold a sale of unwanted books and games to raise money for the local children's hospital. You have asked your English teacher, Mrs Grainger, to help you. Read Mrs Grainger's email and the notes you have made. Then write a reply to Mrs Grainger, using **all** your notes.

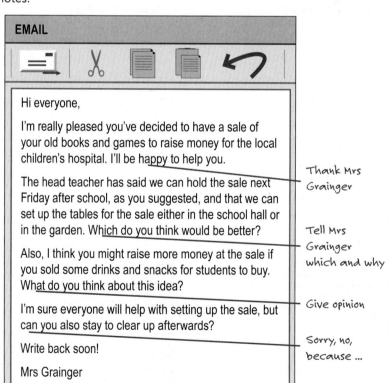

EMAIL

Hi everyone,

I'm really pleased you've decided to have a sale of your old books and games to raise money for the local children's hospital. I'll be happy to help you.

The head teacher has said we can hold the sale next Friday after school, as you suggested, and that we can set up the tables for the sale either in the school hall or in the garden. Which do you think would be better?

Also, I think you might raise more money at the sale if you sold some drinks and snacks for students to buy. What do you think about this idea?

I'm sure everyone will help with setting up the sale, but can you also stay to clear up afterwards?

Write back soon!

Mrs Grainger

Thank Mrs Grainger

Tell Mrs Grainger which and why

Give opinion

Sorry, no, because ...

2 Find the four prompts from the email in the box below. Underline them.

	Prompts	Phrases to use
Responding positively	Yes! Great! Good! Me too!	*What a fantastic idea! It's great you can … Wonderful news! I was pleased to hear …*
Thanking	Thank X	*Thanks for agreeing to … Thank you very much for … Thanks for inviting me to …*
Stating opinion or preference	Give opinion Explain Tell X (which and why) Say which and why	*In my opinion/view, For me … / As for me, I think / believe / feel that … I'd prefer to … / I'd rather … I prefer -ing to -ing It would be better to …*
Giving reasons	Yes/no, because …	*I'd like to / I want to … because I think it will be interesting / great fun / enjoyable. Sorry, I'd love to …, but I've already arranged to … I'm afraid I can't because …*
Suggesting and recommending	Suggest … . Recommend … .	*I suggest …-ing. Why don't we …? How about …-ing? We could always … Why not try … -ing? I'd recommend … -ing.*
Apologising	Apologise Say sorry to … .	*I'm really sorry but … Sorry for (not) …-ing. I'd like to apologise for (not) …-ing.*
Making requests and offers	Ask X to … Offer to …	*Do you think you could …? Could you possibly …? Could you …, please? I could … if you'd like me to. Can I … for you? Shall I …? Would you like me to …?*
Asking questions	Ask X about … .	*Can I/we …? Do I/we …? Should I/we …? Do we have to …? Do you know if / whether / when …? Can you tell me if / whether / when …?*

3 Now read this candidate's answer and the points below it. Answer the questions in *italics*.

Dear Mrs Grainger,
Thank you very much for saying you will help us with our book and game sale. None of us have organised a sale before, so we really need some help.
I think it would be better to hold the sale in the garden, because the weather is sunny. If the students get the chance to hang around and chat outside, they might buy more books and games!
I think we should offer everyone some cold soft drinks; we'll make more money that way. We could offer some cakes and biscuits too. Perhaps some of the students doing a catering course could make some and sell them with the drinks?
I'm really sorry, but I won't be able to stay very long after the sale. I've got a piano lesson on Friday at 4.15. I'll help with everything else though.
Best wishes
Joanna
[145 words]

This is a good answer because Joanna has
- understood the situation correctly.
- responded to all four notes in an appropriate way and in an appropriate style.
- expanded on at least two of the notes. *How has she done this?*
- used a good range of verbs and verb forms. *Which ones? Underline them.*
- begun and ended her reply appropriately.

Beginning and ending an email or letter
You can begin and end emails and letters in the same way.
Informal style: writing to a close friend, another young person, or a member of your family
Begin with: *Hello, Hi* or *Dear* + first name
End with: *Best wishes, All the best, Love*

Semi-formal/formal style: writing to an older person you don't know
Begin with: *Dear* + *Mr/Mrs/Miss* + surname
End with: *Yours* or *Yours sincerely* + your full name

Here are some phrases to start your email/letter:
Informal: *Great news/idea/plan! I'm really pleased for you!*
Semi-formal: *It was great to hear from you. / Thanks so much for your invitation. / I'm really looking forward to …*

Formal: *I was pleased to receive your email/ letter about …*

Some phrases to end your email/letter:
Informal: *I've got to dash now. / That's all for now.*
Semi-formal: *Write soon. / Looking forward to seeing you soon. / Give my best wishes to your family.*
Formal: *I look forward to hearing from you again/soon.*

Writing Part 2

You have a choice of four questions in Part 2 and you only have to answer one of them. Questions 2, 3 and 4 will be three of these: story, review, report, article, informal letter, essay.

Questions 5A and 5B will be on the chosen set texts/films. They may be in the form of an essay, article, report, letter or review. You should only attempt one of these questions if you have studied the relevant book.

Choosing your question and planning your answer

Read through the questions and decide which one you want to answer.
Avoid a question if:

- you don't understand it, or are unsure about what you must do.
- you don't have the necessary vocabulary.
- you don't have enough ideas to write about.

When you have chosen the question:

- underline the important words in it.
- get your ideas together and make a plan. You can do this as a map or diagram, or simply a list of points. There is an example of this on page 64.
- do not start writing until you have a clear plan to work from.

Story

(See Unit 2 page 20.)
Practice task and model answer

1 Read the exam question below and underline the important words. Then answer the questions.

1 Who is the story for? Where will it be read?
2 Over what period of time does the story take place?
3 Do the events in the story have to be positive? Were they planned or not?

> Your English teacher has asked you to write a story for the school website.
> Your story must begin with these words:
> *I was expecting to have a very quiet day, but it turned out to be exactly the opposite.*
> Write your **story**.

2 Now read this candidate's answer and the points below it. Answer the questions in *italics*.

How we became local heroes
I was expecting to have a very quiet day, but it turned out to be exactly the opposite. It was Saturday morning and I was reading sleepily when the phone rang. 'Come quickly, Sam, I need your help!' It was my best friend George, so I couldn't refuse. 'Where are you?' I asked. 'I'm at home, watching the house opposite through my binoculars. Come quickly, through the back garden.'

I rushed round. George told me there was a robbery going on. A large van had driven up and the TV and all the kitchen equipment were being removed. 'But George, there's a much simpler explanation,' I said impatiently. 'They must be moving house.' 'Don't be silly! You know Simon's in our class. He would have said something if his family had been moving!' I realised he was right.

So we phoned the police, who arrived very rapidly. Simon's parents were so relieved and happy that we had stopped the burglary that they took us out for a pizza that night. And by Monday we were famous, because our picture appeared in the paper under the heading 'Local heroes!'. [188 words]

This is a good answer because:

- the story follows well from the prompt sentence, and it is easy to follow what happens.
- it is clearly organised, divided into paragraphs and well punctuated.
- the candidate has used several different past tenses very effectively. *Which ones? Underline them.*
- the story contains some direct speech. *Highlight it. Who is speaking and why is it effective here?*
- the candidate has used a good range of vocabulary and expressions. *Underline some that you think are effective.*
- the candidate has given the story a title. *Why?*

Review

(See Unit 3 page 23.)
Reviews may be on a wide range of topics, and not just on films or books.

Practice task and model answer

1 Read the exam question below and underline the important words. Then answer the questions.

1 Who is the review for?
2 Where will it be read?
3 What sort of website do you have to write about?
4 Do you have to recommend it?

> You have seen this notice in an English-language internet magazine for teenagers.
>
> ### Reviews wanted!   My favourite website
>
> Have you got a favourite website that you spend a lot of time on?
>
> Write us a review of it. Describe the website, explain why you spend a lot of time on it **and** say whether you would recommend it to other people.
>
> The best reviews will be posted in the magazine next month.
>
> Write your **review**.

2 Now read this candidate's answer and the points below it. Answer the questions in *italics*.

My favourite website
The best website I have been on is called UltimateGuitar.com. I spend lots of time on it because I'm learning to play the electric guitar and everything I need is on this site.

It has reviews of all kinds of guitar music, which means jazz and classical as well as pop, rock and so on, so there is something for different tastes. In addition, there is always news and gossip about well-known guitarists. And better still, there are really good interviews to watch, with rock stars, classical guitarists and so on. However, the most fantastic thing about the site is that you can download tabs for all your favourite guitar music from it. It has all the famous riffs and they add new music every week. It's such a popular feature that there is sometimes a queue for downloading. I set it up before school, so it's there when I get home.

I love this website, and I would recommend it to other guitar fans, especially if they are players themselves. And even if you don't play, I'm sure you will find it interesting!
[184 words]

This is a good answer because:

- the candidate has dealt with all the points, giving a clear description of the website and recommending it.
- it is well organised and clearly divided into paragraphs.

- it is well-linked. *Underline the linking words and phrases.*
- it contains different verb tenses. *Which ones? Underline them.*
- it contains a good range of vocabulary about music and websites. *Highlight some.*

Report

(See Unit 5 page 45.)
Reports can be on a wide range of topics, but they are designed so that you can answer them from your own knowledge and personal experience. No specialised knowledge, invented statistics or references to questionnaires or surveys are expected.

Practice task and model answer

1 Read the exam question below and underline the important words. Then answer the questions.

1 Who is the report for?
2 How many points are there to cover?
3 Can you write about any town?

> A group of English students is coming to study at your school. Your teacher has asked you to write a report for them on your local town. You should include information about what there is to see in the town, what shops there are and what you think they will like about the town.
> Write your **report**.

2 Now read this candidate's answer and the points below it. Answer the questions in *italics*.

Report on the town of Pisa
Introduction
Pisa is a very old historic town. There is also some industry in the area, which provides employment for local people who do not work in tourism.
Things to see
The most famous sight in my town is the Leaning Tower of Pisa, which is hundreds of years old and really beautiful. On the same 'Field of Miracles' you also have a cathedral, and two very interesting museums to explore. There are also some attractive gardens near the river. In the old part of town, nearly every building is worth looking at, although some of them need restoring.
Shopping
There is one long street with shops and a department store. Some of the shops are expensive designer places, but there are also cheaper stores selling clothes for young people, and some markets where you can buy real bargains like shoes, bags and jewellery.
What you will enjoy
Pisa is a friendly place and young people spend a lot of time just walking and chatting with their friends and going to outdoor cafés. You will find the atmosphere very relaxing.
[186 words]

This is a good answer because:
- the candidate has dealt with all the points in the question.
- it is well organised under different headings, with an introduction, and one heading for each of the points. *What is the candidate doing in the introduction?*
- it has an appropriate range of vocabulary related to the town and shopping. *Underline some.*
- it is suitable for students. *Why?*

Article

(See Unit 6 page 49.)
Articles can be on a very wide range of topics, and can include some that are not found in other question types, such as colours or flowers. However, you will also find articles on topics that you do find in other question types, for example, sport, friends or food. You can use a more lively and personal style in an article than in some of the other Part 2 questions, and include questions and amusing comments if you wish.

Practice task and model answer

1 **Read the exam question below and underline the important words. Then answer the questions.**

1 Where will the article appear?
2 Who will read it?
3 Do you have to use the three suggestions?

> You see this announcement in an international teenage magazine.
>
> **Articles wanted!**
>
> **The Moon**
> Beautiful evenings? Space travel?
> Poems and songs?
> What does the moon mean to you?
> Write us an article explaining what you feel about the moon and why.
> The best articles will be published in the magazine next month.
>
> Write your **article**.

2 **Now read this candidate's answer and the points below it. Answer the questions in *italics*.**

> What the moon means to me …
> The moon has been important to humans since prehistoric times. I spend hours looking at the night sky, the moon, and the stars. I love the moon, especially when it is full and bright. That's not because I believe in vampires and other scary things that are supposed to appear when the moon is full, but because it is one of the most beautiful things I've ever seen! That is what the moon means to me – beauty.
> Looking at the moon also makes me think about the astronauts who landed there in the 1960s, so the moon connects me to space travel and scientific progress. I have even read science fiction stories about humans living on the moon, but how would we breathe? We would have to live in an artificial atmosphere, which would be horrible.
> Finally, the moon also reminds me of childhood stories. There were often pictures of the moon in them, with cute little animals looking up at it! Now I'm older, I've heard all the old songs about the moon, and love and romance, and of course I've read poems about it too ….
> [189 words]

This is a good answer because:
- the candidate has answered the question well, using some of the suggestions.
- it is well planned and divided into paragraphs. *How? Write the candidate's plan.*
- it contains different verb tenses. *Which ones? Underline them.*

Informal letter

(See Unit 7 page 57.)
Informal letters usually ask you to give information and opinions to a friend who is doing a project or wants advice. You should not write a long introduction with lots of news and chat, but go straight into the main topic. The topic will be something connected to your knowledge of your own country and/or personal experience.

Practice task and model answer

1 **Read the exam question below and underline the important words. Then answer the questions.**

1 Who is going to read your letter?
2 Can you write about any city?
3 You have to write about the history of the city. Can you write about anything else?

> This is part of a letter you have received from your English friend Hannah. Read the letter and write your reply.
>
> *… and we're doing a project on capital cities in my history class. Could you write and tell me something about your capital city and its history and what you would recommend a tourist from another country to visit?*
> *Thanks a lot – and write soon.*
> *Best wishes, Hannah*
>
> Write your **letter**.

2 Now read this candidate's answer and the points below it. Answer the questions in *italics*.

Dear Hannah,
Your history project sounds fascinating!
Paris has a long and interesting history, going back to Roman times. The oldest part is the Île de la Cité, where the Romans first settled, and then the French kings built the Sainte-Chappelle, the Conciergerie prison and the wonderful cathedral of Notre Dame there a thousand years later. These monuments are still there, but in the nineteenth century a famous architect called Baron Haussmann pulled down many of the houses around them to make way for new buildings which everyone now thinks of as being typical of Paris.
I think the one place you must see is the Louvre. Before the French Revolution it was a royal palace; it's a fantastic building, and it contains the famous picture of the Mona Lisa, and wonderful statues. The Louvre is enormous; there is too much to see in a lifetime! When you are tired, you can always go to the Latin Quarter, the student area where there are lots of little restaurants, or walk by the beautiful river Seine and look at the views of the Eiffel Tower from a pavement café.
 Best wishes,
 Andrea
[191 words]

This is a good answer because:
- the candidate has answered the question well, writing in an interesting way about the capital city, its history and places to visit. *Underline the historical facts mentioned and highlight the places you can visit.*
- the letter is well organised and divided into paragraphs, and sentences are well structured.
- the candidate has started and ended the letter with friendly phrases. *Underline them.*

Essay

(See Unit 8 page 64.)
Essays always ask you to give your opinion, and you will need to give examples to support your ideas and to explain why you hold these views. Sometimes it's helpful to explain views that you disagree with and give reasons for your disagreement. You will be able to answer the question from your own knowledge and experience. No specialised knowledge is required.

Practice task and model answer

1 Read the exam question below and underline the important words. Then answer the questions.

1 Who is the essay for?
2 Do you have to write about both languages and science subjects?

3 Can you write about any other subjects?
4 Can you say anything you like in the conclusion?

> You have had a discussion in your English class about school subjects. Now your teacher has asked you to write an essay answering this question for homework:
> *Is it more useful to study several foreign languages or to study several science subjects at school?*
> Write your **essay**.

2 Now read this candidate's answer and the points below it. Answer the questions in *italics*.

I would like to start my essay by saying that whether languages or sciences are more useful depends very much on what job you would like to do. If you want to be a doctor or a nurse, or a great inventor, of course you will need to study science subjects, like biology, physics and chemistry. However, I would argue that there really isn't much point in studying science subjects if you are going to be a history teacher, or work in a shop.
On the other hand, learning languages is always useful, whatever job you want to do in the future, and whatever subject you want to study at university. Of course, English is very useful because so many people speak it, but other languages, like Spanish and Chinese, are also becoming very important.
Therefore, I would like to conclude by saying that, ideally, everyone should study several foreign languages, simply because they are useful in every job. It is good to study science as well, but not many people will become experts in it. For many people, and that includes me, science beyond a certain level is very difficult, although it's good to have a basic knowledge.
[199 words]

This is a good answer because:
- the candidate has answered the question well, talking about both science subjects and foreign languages.
- it is well organised into paragraphs. *How? Write the candidate's plan.*
- the candidate has come to a definite conclusion. *What is it?*
- it is easy to read and well-linked. *Underline the linking phrases.*

Set texts

There is one question on each of two set texts. You may answer the question from your knowledge of the book, or a film based on the book. For this question you need knowledge of the book or film, the main characters and the main events of the story. You may be asked to write an essay, article, letter, report or review, although essays are the most common.
The book titles change every two years, and information can be found on the CESOL website (www.cambridgeesol.org).

verb	past simple	past participle	verb	past simple	past participle
arise	arose	arisen	hear	heard	heard
be	was/were	been	hide	hid	hidden
beat	beat	beaten	hit	hit	hit
become	became	become	hold	held	held
begin	began	begun	hurt	hurt	hurt
bend	bent	bent	keep	kept	kept
bite	bit	bitten	kneel	knelt	knelt
bleed	bled	bled	know	knew	known
blow	blew	blown	lay	laid	laid
break	broke	broken	lead	led	led
bring	brought	brought	lean	leant/ leaned	leant/ leaned
broadcast	broadcast	broadcast			
build	built	built	learn	learnt/ learned	learnt/ learned
burn	burnt/ burned	burnt/ burned	leave	left	left
burst	burst	burst	lend	lent	lent
buy	bought	bought	let	let	let
catch	caught	caught	lie	lay	lain
choose	chose	chosen	light	lit	lit
come	came	come	lose	lost	lost
cost	cost	cost	make	made	made
creep	crept	crept	mean	meant	meant
cut	cut	cut	meet	met	met
deal	dealt	dealt	pay	paid	paid
dig	dug	dug	put	put	put
do	did	done	read	read	read
draw	drew	drawn	ride	rode	ridden
dream	dreamt/ dreamed	dreamt/ dreamed	ring	rang	rung
			rise	rose	risen
drink	drank	drunk	run	ran	run
drive	drove	driven	say	said	said
eat	ate	eaten	see	saw	seen
fall	fell	fallen	sell	sold	sold
feed	fed	fed	send	sent	sent
feel	felt	felt	set	set	set
fight	fought	fought	sew	sewed	sewn
find	found	found	shake	shook	shaken
fly	flew	flown	shine	shone	shone
forbid	forbade	forbidden	shoot	shot	shot
forget	forgot	forgotten	show	showed	shown
forgive	forgave	forgiven	shrink	shrank	shrunk
freeze	froze	frozen	shut	shut	shut
get	got	got	sing	sang	sung
give	gave	given	sink	sank	sunk
go	went	gone/been	sit	sat	sat
grow	grew	grown	sleep	slept	slept
hang	hung	hung	slide	slid	slid
have	had	had	smell	smelt/ smelled	smelt/ smelled

verb	past simple	past participle
sow	sowed	sown
speak	spoke	spoken
spell	spelt/ spelled	spelt/ spelled
spend	spent	spent
spill	spilt/ spilled	spilt/ spilled
spit	spat	spat
split	split	split
spoil	spoilt/ spoiled	spoilt/ spoiled
spread	spread	spread
spring	sprang	sprung
stand	stood	stood
steal	stole	stolen
stick	stuck	stuck
sting	stung	stung
strike	struck	struck
swear	swore	sworn
sweep	swept	swept
swell	swelled	swollen
swim	swam	swum
swing	swung	swung
take	took	taken
teach	taught	taught
tear	tore	torn
tell	told	told
think	thought	thought
throw	threw	thrown
understand	understood	understood
wake	woke	woken
wear	wore	worn
weep	wept	wept
win	won	won
write	wrote	written

WORDLIST

Unit 1

approach *n* a way of doing something

approval *n* when you think that something or someone is good or right

arrogant *adj* believing that you are better than other people

at all *exp* in any way or of any type (used to make negatives and questions stronger)

at last *exp* finally

at least *exp* as much as, or more than, a number or amount

at once *exp* immediately

be put off *pv* to have your attention taken away from something you are doing

believe in *v* to be confident that something is effective and right

bold *adj* brave

celebrate *v* to have a party or a nice meal because it is a special day or something good has happened

community *n* the people living in a particular area

daylight *n* the natural light from the sun during the day

demand *v* a strong request or need for something

depend on *v* to need the help and support of someone or something

doubtful *adj* If you are doubtful about something, you are uncertain about it.

eager *adj* wanting to do or have something very much

energetic *adj* having or needing a lot of energy

expect (someone to do something) *v* to think that someone should behave in a particular way or do a particular thing

formal *adj* not casual, official

get away with *pv* to succeed in avoiding punishment for something

impatient *adj* If you are impatient, you get angry with people who make mistakes or you hate waiting for things.

irritated *adj* annoyed

jealous *adj* not happy because you want something that someone else has

make a comparison *exp* to compare two or more things

prompt *n* a note which helps or assists in a task

relieved *adj* feeling happy because something bad did not happen

significant *adj* important

spot *n* a place

thrilling *adj* very exciting

tradition *n* a custom or way of behaving that has continued for a long time in a group of people

weird *adj* very strange

My words

....
....
....
....
....
....
....
....
....
....

Unit 2

accidental *adj* by chance

adventurous *adj* liking to try new or difficult things

aggressive *adj* angry and violent towards another person

attempt *n* when you try to do something

aware *adj* knowing about something

bearable *adj* If an unpleasant situation is bearable, you can accept or deal with it.

clumsy *adj* Clumsy people move in a way that is not controlled or careful, and often knock or damage things.

confidence *n* when you are certain of your ability to do things well

considerable *adj* large or important enough to have an effect

controversial *adj* causing a lot of disagreement or argument

courageous *adj* brave

decisive *adj* making decisions quickly and easily

desirable *adj* If something is desirable, it is very good or attractive and most people would want it.

disappearance *n* when someone or something suddenly goes somewhere and is impossible to see or find

disaster *n* a very bad situation, especially something that causes a lot of harm or damage

draw attention to *exp* to bring people's notice to something

explorer *n* someone who travels to places where no one has ever been in order to find out what is there

furious *adj* very angry

get into trouble *exp* to get into problems or difficulties, or to be punished for something

highlight *v* to emphasise something or make people notice something

hold your breath *exp* to stop breathing

industrial *adj* connected with industry

injury *n* damage to someone's body

judgement *n* the ability to form valuable opinions and make good decisions

logical *adj* using reason

mysterious *adj* strange and not explained or understood

optimistic *adj* always thinking that good things will happen

predictable *adj* happening or behaving in a way that you expect and not unusual or interesting

rapid *adj* happening or moving very quickly

remarkable *adj* very unusual in a way that you admire

rural *adj* relating to the countryside and not to towns

universal *adj* relating to everyone in the world, or to everyone in a particular group

warning *n* something that tells or shows you that something bad may happen

My words

....
....
....
....
....
....
....
....
....
....

Unit 3

appeal *v* to attract or interest someone

be supposed to (do something) *v* to have to, should (do something)

cast *n* all the actors in a film or play

character *n* a person in a book, film, etc.

contain *v* If one thing contains another, it has it inside it.

costume *n* all the clothes that you wear at the same time, usually special clothes

determined *adj* wanting so much to do something that you keep trying very hard

direction *n* the control of a film, play, etc.

distinguish *v* to see or understand the differences between two people, ideas, or things

emotion *n* a strong feeling such as love or anger

exceptional *adj* very good and better than most other people or things

have trouble (doing something) *exp* to experience difficulties in doing something

hero *n* the main character in a book or film

impressive *adj* Someone or something that is impressive makes you admire and respect them.

justice *n* treatment of people that is fair

lyrics *n* the words of a song

outstanding *adj* excellent and much better than most

personality *n* the qualities that make one person different from another

play a part *exp* to take a role in a film, play, etc.

plot *n* the things that happen in a story

producer *n* someone who controls how a film, play, programme, or musical recording is made

reaction *n* something you say, feel, or do because of something that has happened

review *n* a piece of writing in a newspaper that gives an opinion about a new book, film, etc.

romantic comedy *n* a film which combines a comedy with a love story

schedule *n* a plan that tells you when things will happen

script *n* the words in a film, play, etc.

set *n* the place where a film or play is performed or recorded and the pictures, furniture, etc. that are used

shot *n* a short piece in a film in which there is a single action or a short series of actions

special effects *n* an unusual type of action in a film, or an entertainment on stage, created by using special equipment

stand out *pv* to be very noticeable

stunt *n* when someone does something dangerous that needs great skill, usually in a film

symbol *n* a sign or object that is used to mean something

My words

....
....
....
....
....
....
....
....
....
....
....

Unit 4

athletics *n* the sports which include running, jumping and throwing

(a) balanced diet *exp* a diet that contains the right amounts of different types of food

benefit *v* to have a helpful or good effect on someone or something

benefit *n* a helpful or good effect

convenience *n* when something is easy to use and suitable for what you want to do

curiosity *n* the feeling of wanting to know or learn about something

decoration *n* when you make something look more attractive by putting things on it, or something that you use to do this

defender *n* someone in a sports team who tries to prevent the other team from scoring points, goals, etc.

division *n* when something is separated into parts or groups

equality *n* when everyone is equal and has the same rights, etc.

generosity *n* the quality of being generous

get involved in *exp* to take part in something

independence *n* when someone looks after themselves and does not need help from other people

informal *adj* suitable for when you are with friends or family, but not for official occasions

keep fit *exp* to remain healthy and strong, usually as a result of exercise

lap *n* one journey around a race track

martial arts *n* sports that are traditional Japanese or Chinese forms of fighting or defending yourself, e.g. judo, karate

opponent *n* someone who you compete against in a game or competition

patience *n* when you are able to stay calm and not get angry, especially when something takes a long time

penalty *n* in sports, an advantage given to a team when the other team has broken a rule, e.g. in football, a kick straight at the goal

pitch *n* an area of ground where a sport is played

potential *adj* A potential problem, employer, partner, etc. may become one in the future, although they are not one now.

production *n* the process of making or growing goods to be sold

professional *n* Someone is a professional if they get money for a sport or activity which most people do as a hobby.

pudding *n* in the UK, sweet food that is usually eaten as the last part of a meal

react *v* to say, do or feel something because of something else that has been said or done

referee *n* someone who makes sure that players follow the rules during a sports game

responsible (for) *adj* having control and authority over something or someone and the duty of taking care of it or them

similarity *n* when two things or people are similar, or a way in which they are similar

tackle *n* when you try to get the ball from someone in a game like football

track *n* a path, often circular, used for races

umpire *n* someone whose job is to watch a sports game and make sure that the players obey the rules

My words

....
....
....
....
....
....
....
....
....
....

abolish *v* to end a law or system

adapt *v* to change for a new situation

appreciate *v* to feel grateful for something

canteen *n* a restaurant in an office, factory or school

capable *adj* able to do things well

combine *v* to become mixed or joined, or to mix or join things together

come across *pv* to find or meet by chance

come down with *pv* to start to suffer from an illness, especially one that is not serious

come up with *pv* to suggest or think of an idea or plan

communicative *adj* willing to talk to people and give them information

competitive *adj* wanting to win or be better than other people

construction *n* the work of building houses, offices, bridges, etc.

demanding *adj* needing a lot of your time, attention or effort

enthusiastic *adj* keen, eager, showing enthusiasm

facilities *n* buildings or equipment that are provided for a particular purpose

give up *pv* to stop doing a particular activity or job

go off *pv* to stop liking or being interested in someone or something

go over *pv* to examine or look at something in a careful or detailed way

go through *pv* to experience a difficult or unpleasant situation

look down on *pv* to think that someone is less important than you

set *n* a group of pupils at school who have a similar level in a particular subject

shelter *n* a place that protects you from bad weather or danger

sports kit *n* the clothes that pupils wear to play sports at school

state school *n* a school that is free to go to because the government provides the money for it

(be) streamed *v* (relating to school pupils of a similar level, age and intelligence) to be grouped together

sympathetic *adj* showing that you understand and care about someone's problems

thorough *adj* careful and covering every detail

volunteer *n* someone who works without being paid, especially work that involves helping people

My words

....

....

....

....

....

....

....

....

....

....

Unit 6

air conditioning *n* a system that keeps the air cool in a building or car

be green *exp* to be interested in protecting the environment

bush *n* a short, thick plant with a lot of branches

climate change *n* the way the Earth's weather is changing

environment *n* the air, water and land in or on which people, animals and plants live

erupt *v* If a volcano erupts, it suddenly throws out fire and melted rocks.

flooding *n* when the land becomes covered with water, especially in a way that causes problems

fuel *n* a substance that is burned to give heat or power

humid *adj* Humid air or weather is hot and slightly wet.

hurricane *n* a violent storm with very strong winds

litter *n* pieces of paper and other waste that are left in public places

mild *adj* When the weather in winter is mild, it is not cold.

packaged (food) *adj* in boxes or containers to be sold

pine tree *n* an evergreen (= never losing its leaves) tree that grows in cooler areas of the world

pollution *n* damage caused to water, air, etc. by bad substances or waste

pressure *n* difficult situations that make you feel worried or unhappy

purchase *v* to buy something

rainfall *n* the amount of rain that falls in a particular place at a particular time

ready meals *n* prepared meals that are often already cooked and just need to be heated up

recycle *v* to use paper, glass, plastic, etc. again and not throw it away

rubbish *n* things that you throw away because you do not want them

shortage *n* when there is not enough of something

submit *v* to send a document, plan, etc. to someone so that they can consider it

transport *n* when people or things are moved from one place to another

volcano *n* a mountain with a large hole at the top which sometimes explodes

My words

....
....
....
....
....
....
....
....
....

admire *v* to like or respect someone or something because they are good or clever

amused *adj* showing that you think something is funny

ashamed *adj* feeling bad because you have done something wrong

be keen on *exp* to be very interested in something

belief *n* when you believe that something is true or real

can't bear *exp* to strongly dislike someone or something

casual *adj* Casual clothes are comfortable and not formal.

(feel) cheated *exp* to feel that you have been prevented from obtaining or achieving something

concerned *adj* worried

conventional *adj* Conventional objects or ways of doing things are the usual ones which have been used for a long time.

deliberate *adj* If an action is deliberate, you wanted or planned to do it.

discouraged *adj* having lost your confidence in something or your enthusiasm for it

drag *v* to pull something or someone somewhere, usually with difficulty

elegant *adj* stylish and attractive

expectation *n* when you expect something to happen (often something good)

fate *n* what happens to a particular person or thing, especially something negative

freedom *n* the right to live in the way you want without being controlled by anyone else

gaze *n* a long look at someone or something

keep up with *pv* If you keep up with something or someone, you stay at the same level as it or them.

lean (on) *v* to move the top part of your body in a particular direction

on the other hand *exp* (usually following *on the one hand*) used to compare two different facts or opinions on a situation

outrageous *adj* shocking or extreme

passionate *adj* showing a strong feeling about a subject

second-hand *adj* If something is second-hand, someone else had it or used it before you.

shocking *adj* very bad and making you feel upset

show off *pv* to behave in a way that is intended to attract attention

to take no notice of *exp* not to give attention to someone or something

upset *adj* sad or worried because something bad has happened

vintage *adj* having all the best or most typical qualities of something, especially from the past

whereas *conj* compared with the fact that

My words

....
....
....
....
....
....
....
....
....
....

Unit 8

absorb *v* to understand and remember something

accessible *adj* easy to understand, find or reach

atom *n* the smallest unit that an element can be divided into

attachment *n* a computer file which is sent together with an email message

automatically *adv* If a machine or device does something automatically, it does it independently, without human control

back up *pv* to make an extra copy of computer information, e.g. your work

bookmark *n* an address on the internet that you record so that you can quickly find something again

cell *n* the smallest living part of an animal or a plant

claim *v* to say that something is true

concept *n* an idea or principle

conservation *n* the protection of nature

crucial *adj* extremely important or necessary

desktop *n* a computer that is small enough to fit on a desk

extensive *adj* large in amount or size

hard drive *n* the part inside a computer that is not removed and stores very large amounts of information

identify *v* to recognise a problem, need, fact, etc. and to show that it exists

(be/get) inspired *adj* having ideas from someone or something

investigate *v* to try to get all the facts about something

log in/on *pv* to connect a computer to a computer system by typing your name, so that you can start work

log off/out *pv* to stop a computer being connected to a computer system, usually when you want to stop working

monitor *n* a screen that shows information or pictures, usually connected to a computer

necessity *n* something that you need

pedal *v* to push the pedals of a bicycle round with your feet

percentage *n* an amount of something, expressed as a number out of 100

play a trick (on) *exp* to deceive or cheat someone as a joke

reveal *v* to tell or show someone a piece of (secret) information

self-conscious *adj* too aware of what other people are thinking about you and your appearance

survival *n* when someone or something continues to live, especially after a dangerous situation

technical *adj* relating to the knowledge, machines, or methods used in science and industry

vast *adj* very big

vital *adj* necessary

My words

....

....

....

....

....

....

....

....

....

Reading • Part 1

Questions 1–8

You are going to read an extract from a book about how people succeed in sport. For questions **1–8**, choose the answer (**A**, **B**, **C** or **D**) which you think fits best according to the text.

Mark your answers **on the separate answer sheet**.

Path to the top

Matthew Syed talks about how he became a table tennis star

At the age of 24, I became the British number-one table tennis player for the very first time which, I am sure you will agree, is a huge achievement. I suddenly found myself on the receiving end of regular invitations to speak to school audiences about my rise to international glory, and would often take my gold medals along to show the youngsters.

Table tennis is a pretty big sport in the UK, with 2.4 million participants, thousands of teams, and serious riches for those who do well. But what made me special? What had marked me out for sporting greatness? I came up with a number of factors: speed, determination, mental strength, adaptability, agility and reflexes. Sometimes I would marvel at the fact that I had these skills in such large amounts that they were capable of raising me – little me! – beyond hundreds of thousands of
line 15 others aiming for that precious top spot. And all this was doubly amazing, considering I had been born into a family in an ordinary suburb of an ordinary town in south-east England. I had no particular advantages. Mine was a triumph of individuality; a personal journey of success against the odds.

This, of course, is the way that many who have reached the top in sport, or indeed in any other field, choose to tell their stories. Many of us live in a culture that encourages this kind of individualism. The film world of Hollywood is full of such narratives, often sugar-coated with emotion. But while these stories are inspirational, and compulsively entertaining, are they true? Here is my story in table tennis.

When I was eight years old my parents, for reasons they are still unable to explain (neither of them plays table tennis), decided to buy a table tennis table and to put it in our large garage. I don't know the exact percentage, but you can imagine that there were not many youngsters of my age in my home town who possessed a full-size, tournament-specification table. Fewer still had a garage in which it could be housed full-time. This was my first bit of good fortune.

My second piece of good fortune was having an older brother called Andrew who came to love table tennis as much as I did. We would play for hours in the garage after school: duelling, battling, testing each other's reflexes, experimenting with new spins, investigating new rackets, inviting over friends who, although often more able in other sports, were surprised to see just how far we had advanced in table tennis. Without knowing it, we were happily acquiring thousands of hours of practice.

Mr Charters was a teacher at the local primary school, Aldryngton. He was the coach of almost all the after-school sporting clubs, the manager of the school football team, the caretaker of the badminton equipment and the organiser of school sports day. But Charters cared about one thing above all: table tennis. He was the nation's top coach and a
line 35 senior figure in the English Table Tennis Association. The other sports were just a front, an opportunity to search out sporting talent wherever it emerged so he could focus it – determinedly and exclusively – upon table tennis.

For a period, the streets around Silverdale Road, where the school was situated, produced more outstanding table tennis players than the rest of the nation combined. It seemed to go against explanation or belief. Had something spread genetically throughout the local neighbourhood without touching the surrounding roads or villages? Of course not: the success of Silverdale Road was about the coming together of factors of a similar kind to those that have, from time to time, happened in other parts of the world. In particular, all of the sporting talent was focused entirely on table tennis, and all of the potential players were encouraged by an outstanding coach. And as for me, with a table in the garage and a brother as passionate about table tennis as myself, I had a head start before I even got to Aldryngton School.

1 In the first paragraph, the writer says that he
   A had not realised how hard he would have to work to get to the top.
   B wanted to make the right impression on other young people.
   C had not expected to be asked to talk about himself.
   D arranged to talk to as many young people as he could.

2 What does 'all this' refer to in line 15?
   A the number of people who play table tennis
   B the amount of time the writer took to improve his skills
   C the amount of money earned by table tennis players
   D the level of success the writer has achieved

3 Why does the writer compare his story to those that are told in films?
   A to illustrate the interest in stories of people succeeding through their own talents
   B to suggest that the stories of real people can be made into good films
   C to complain that film-makers are not so interested in the stories of sports people
   D to show the importance of realising that everybody has a unique story to tell

4 The writer refers to the purchase of the table tennis table as 'good fortune' because
   A his parents only bought it because they recognised his talents.
   B it was not a logical item for his parents to spend their money on.
   C the garage was only just big enough for it to fit in.
   D it was an unusual hobby for a boy to have at the time.

5 Why did the brothers spend so much time playing table tennis together?
   A They knew by practising a lot they would do well later.
   B They wanted to show their friends how good they were.
   C They knew they weren't good at other sports.
   D They were inspired to compete against each other.

6 What is meant by 'the other sports were just a front' in line 35?
   A The children didn't appreciate Mr Charters' efforts to improve their table tennis.
   B Mr Charters got annoyed that he had to spend time on sports other than table tennis.
   C Mr Charters used other sports to find children who might be good at table tennis.
   D Other sports Mr Charters taught were less popular with the children than table tennis.

7 What point is the writer making in the last paragraph?
   A The fact that Silverdale Road produced so many table tennis players can be explained.
   B Similar circumstances in other parts of the world have not had the same results.
   C It became clear that the success of Silverdale Road could only continue for a short time.
   D The people in surrounding villages wished they had the same sporting facilities.

8 What do we find out about the writer in this text?
   A He wishes he had had the chance to try other sports too.
   B He is grateful for the opportunities which came his way by chance.
   C He is aware that success can take some of the pleasure out of a sport.
   D He realises the importance of not getting emotional about a sport.

Reading • Part 2

Questions 9–15

You are going to read a newspaper article about dinosaurs. Seven sentences have been removed from the article. Choose from the sentences **A–H** the one which fits each gap (**9–15**). There is one sentence which you do not need to use.

Mark your answers **on the separate answer sheet**.

How much do we really know about dinosaurs?

Palaeontologists study fossils, the remains of animals that lived in prehistoric times. Fossils can be between several thousand and hundreds of millions of years old and new technology enables researchers to discover more and more about them. Recently, palaeontologists from Manchester University have found that dinosaurs, usually shown as enormous, earth-shaking monsters, may have been much lighter than previously thought.

Dinosaurs have fascinated people in Britain since the first fragments of their bones emerged from the stone quarries of southern England in the early 1800s, but the scientists working on their remains at the time were faced with a difficult task. **9** ☐ And of course there were no obvious living equivalents.

Nearly 200 years after these initial discoveries, palaeontologists are still trying to resolve the issue of what dinosaurs really looked like. **10** ☐ This is due to new finds and technologies beyond the wildest imaginings of those early scholars who, working by candlelight, eagerly chipped away at their latest discoveries with hammer and chisel.

Initially, dinosaurs were considered to be iguanas (a kind of lizard) on a much larger scale. Nineteenth-century scientists worked out that if dinosaurs had the same proportions as iguanas, then monsters over 60 metres long once existed in Britain. **11** ☐ This point of view remained popular until the first complete dinosaur skeletons were found, first in Europe and then in huge quantities in the American west.

The discoveries of whole skeletons had a lasting effect on all subsequent impressions of dinosaur appearance, revealing for the first time a set of animals that were to become familiar from movies and museum displays, including Stegosaurus, Allosaurus and Diplodocus. It became clear that dinosaurs possessed an amazing variety of body shapes and sizes, from flexible, two-legged meat-eaters to long-necked grass-eating herbivores. **12** ☐ From this time dinosaurs were therefore no longer reconstructed as giant lizards. However, the biology of the 'new' dinosaurs was still compared to that of known living reptiles, and they were still reconstructed as large clumsy beasts.

For much of the 20th century, this impression dominated scientific and public imaginations. Dinosaurs were seen as the ultimate example of a failed species, which became extinct. **13** ☐ In addition, far from being an evolutionary dead end, dinosaurs gave rise to the birds, and we now have fossils showing that dinosaurs were the first to have feathers. All of these discoveries come from the efforts of palaeontologists in the 1970s, which saw a revolution in our understanding of dinosaurs.

These advances mean that we can now work out how well some dinosaurs could hear or smell. **14** ☐ Because of all this extra knowledge, mammals and birds are now viewed as more appropriate models for dinosaur biology, which offers many new insights into their evolution and behaviour.

15 ☐ How exactly did they die out? Why did some of them prosper while others were short-lived? What were the functions of certain bizarre features? And which factors led to their runaway evolutionary success? There are still plenty of things we know nothing about – and scientists shouldn't be afraid to say so.

A But none of these resembled the massive, nightmarish visions imagined only a few years earlier.

B But some things have become much easier, however.

C In fact, the opposite is the case as we now see dinosaurs as highly successful social creatures with complex behaviours.

D We even have an idea of what some of the original colours of dinosaurs might have been.

E But they based their calculations on individual bones alone.

F We are still in the dark, however, when it comes to some aspects of dinosaur life.

G Because of this, they were able to analyse old bones in much greater detail than ever before.

H It was not clear to them how to reconstruct the appearance and behaviour of animals that had been dead for hundreds of millions of years.

Reading • Part 3

Questions 16–30

You are going to read some magazine reviews of video games. For questions **16–30**, choose from the reviews (**A–E**). The reviews may be chosen more than once.

Mark your answers **on the separate answer sheet**.

Which reviewer says

there is a need for the user to be patient at certain points in the game?	16
the game has a storyline which is adequate rather than outstanding?	17
the faults in the way the game sometimes worked have been fixed?	18
the game has similarities to some films with a particular actor in them?	19
the music is a good accompaniment to what is happening in the game?	20
their expectations of the game were too pessimistic?	21
the game might not attract more users despite better graphics?	22
the poor quality of the graphics in some circumstances is understandable?	23
the fact that the tasks are rarely repeated means the game isn't boring?	24
improvements to the graphics have helped recognition of the characters?	25
some of the game's fans have recently been lost to competing games?	26
a vital part is played by the graphics in maintaining the users' interest during the game?	27
the game's appeal is much wider now than its original intended audience?	28
there are characters in the game which the user can relate to?	29
the game will provide new competition for best-selling games?	30

Review of the latest video games by our teenage readers

A *Baseball X2* reviewed by Liam, aged 14

I always thought *Baseball X1* was the coolest sports simulation game that I had ever come across. This version, *Baseball X2*, is an update and has taken everything that I adored and made it even better! It has also put right some of the little things that went wrong during the game. Sports games that have got a much larger share of the market had better look out because this game is going to be big! The graphics were fairly advanced on the earlier version except it was difficult to tell some of the players apart and they looked a bit like aliens, but now they are so realistic you know immediately who they are.

B *Speedy Track 008* reviewed by Leila, aged 16

Speedy Track was a very successful racing game when the first version came out. However, the last version was pretty poor quality, and serious gamers have been moving over to the *Big Prize* and *Monaco* series instead. So will this new version bring them back? Well, the graphics have improved – the roads and scenery are now more detailed. But *Big Prize* and *Monaco* have perfectly good graphics themselves so the debate is open as to which game will appeal most. The game concentrates on a race through the mountains that is filled with crashes and explosions. The idea of this kind of cross-country race is very interesting and has never been properly explored in a video game before, as far as I know. Tom Sapori appeared in an advertising trailer for this game and I can see why. The game has the same kind of action that is in most of his movies. Something about the craziness just draws you in.

C *Dragon* reviewed by Kurt, aged 15

The plot isn't what you would call prize-winning, but it gets you involved immediately and finishes off without any loose ends. A month ago I was afraid that what we might get was another disappointing addition to the series, but after playing on this new version I can't wait to see what will come next. The graphics in the game take your breath away. It's a good thing too, since you spend a lot of time travelling in the game and it would be tiring to have a dull background which was repeated all the time. The music is almost too good as it distracts you from what you're doing. The characters' movements are smooth and the controls are so easy to use.

D *White City* reviewed by Georgia, aged 14

The game's main downside is its graphics. They aren't awful, but they're certainly not the best I've seen. However, the reduced detail isn't surprising due to the fact that at times you can be looking at an entire town from thousands of metres in the air, and then you are immediately down on the ground. The characters are well done though – they all have unique qualities and you feel as if you can actually talk to them. There is one thing gamers will not enjoy. After completing a level, the home screen appears. These dull moments might ruin your concentration, but you just need to put up with them as they only last about a minute, although they feel much longer.

E *Shopper* reviewed by Sofia, aged 12

Shopper allows gamers to stock their own shop and take on the role of a shop-keeper by buying and selling stuff. This was aimed at children at first but the game's charm has proved popular with older people and is becoming a massive hit.

The game is constantly throwing new challenges at you so you need to be concentrating all the time and you will play over and over again. The voices sound crisp and clear. The music is even better – the band Excel has written songs especially to go with different stages of the game and they do a great job. At the end you hear the theme tune from the film 'Wherever' and it's an extremely catchy tune!

Writing • Part 1

You **must** answer this question. Write your answer in **120–150** words in an appropriate style.

1 You have received an email from your English teacher, Mrs Challis. Read Mrs Challis's email and the notes you have made. Then write an email to Mrs Challis, using **all** your notes.

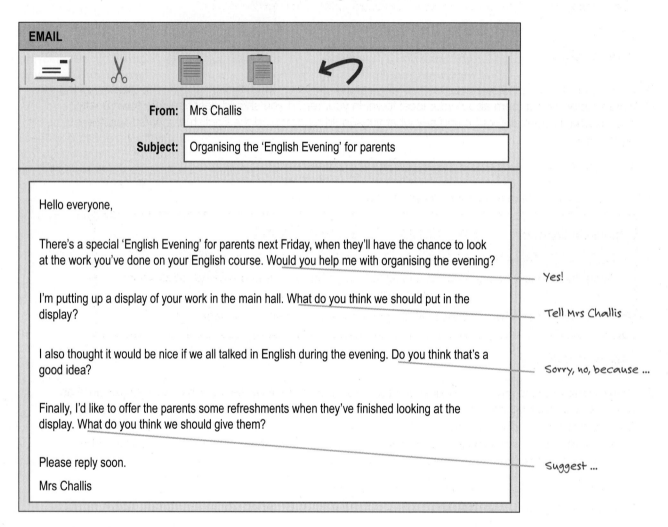

EMAIL

From: Mrs Challis

Subject: Organising the 'English Evening' for parents

Hello everyone,

There's a special 'English Evening' for parents next Friday, when they'll have the chance to look at the work you've done on your English course. Would you help me with organising the evening? ———— Yes!

I'm putting up a display of your work in the main hall. What do you think we should put in the display? ———— Tell Mrs Challis

I also thought it would be nice if we all talked in English during the evening. Do you think that's a good idea? ———— Sorry, no, because ...

Finally, I'd like to offer the parents some refreshments when they've finished looking at the display. What do you think we should give them? ———— Suggest ...

Please reply soon.

Mrs Challis

Write your **email**. You must use grammatically correct sentences with accurate spelling and punctuation in a style appropriate for the situation.

Writing • Part 2

Write an answer to **one** of the questions **2–5** in this part. Write your answer in **120–180** words in an appropriate style. Put the question number in the box at the top of the page.

---

2 You have had a discussion in your English class about the importance of sport. Now your teacher has asked you to write an essay for homework answering the following question:

Is it a good idea for all young people to do sport?

Write your **essay**.

3 Some English students are coming to your school on an exchange visit. Your teacher has asked you to write a report telling them about your local town. In your report you should describe your town briefly, explain what is special about it and say what you would recommend the English students to do there during their visit.

Write your **report**.

4 You have seen this announcement on an international website.

> **Reviews wanted**   **The Best TV Series Ever!**
>
> Do you have a favourite TV series that you watch regularly?
>
> Write us a review telling us what it is about, why you enjoy it and whether other young people would enjoy watching it.
>
> The best reviews will be posted on the website next week.

Write your **review**.

5 Answer **one** of the following two questions based on **one** of the titles below. Write the letter (**a**) or (**b**) as well as the number 5 in the question box.

(a) *Touching the Void* by Joe Simpson

You have had a discussion in your English class about the characters in *Touching the Void*. Now your teacher has given you this essay for homework:

How did Joe Simpson manage to survive in Touching the Void?

Write your **essay**.

(b) *Macbeth* by William Shakespeare

You have seen this notice on an English-language website for young people.

> **Articles wanted**   **An Exciting Opening**
>
> We are looking for articles about stories which start in an exciting way.
>
> The best articles will be posted on the website.

You have decided to write about the opening of *Macbeth*.

Write your **article**.

Use of English • Part 1

For questions **1–12**, read the text below and decide which word (**A**, **B**, **C** or **D**) best fits the gap. There is an example at the beginning (**0**).

Mark your answers **on the separate answer sheet**.

Example:

0   **A** making   **B** forcing   **C** causing   **D** producing

```
0 | A   B   C   D |
  | ▬   ▭   ▭   ▭ |
```

Kites

Nobody can resist the idea of (**0**) .... an object fly through the sky. Kites are flown all around

the world for pleasure and as a (**1**) .... of transporting things and people. It is an interest that

(**2**) .... back thousands of years. The first kites were flown in Asia and by the year 1000 they

played a significant (**3**) .... in many different cultures. For instance, they were sometimes flown

over a house to (**4**) .... the fact that there was a new baby. In some places people (**5**) ....

thought kite-flying could encourage the winds to blow away the rain clouds and (**6**) .... the crops

from flooding. Eventually scientists and inventors began to be (**7**) .... of the potential of kites.

(**8**) .... then large kites have been developed which can pull people and vehicles and lift equipment

up into the air. But kite-flying (**9**) .... a sport which can be enjoyed by people of all ages and it

doesn't (**10**) .... a fortune. All you need is some wind and (**11**) .... a hill or a beach where you

can stand. If you are a beginner, you will probably also need someone to pick the kite up every time it falls

to the (**12**) .... !

1	**A** procedure	**B** technique	**C** means	**D** process
2	**A** gets	**B** goes	**C** stands	**D** comes
3	**A** purpose	**B** function	**C** position	**D** role
4	**A** announce	**B** tell	**C** advise	**D** inform
5	**A** thus	**B** therefore	**C** yet	**D** even
6	**A** maintain	**B** prevent	**C** support	**D** avoid
7	**A** attentive	**B** sensitive	**C** familiar	**D** aware
8	**A** After	**B** Following	**C** Since	**D** Later
9	**A** remains	**B** stays	**C** continues	**D** keeps
10	**A** charge	**B** spend	**C** pay	**D** cost
11	**A** perfectly	**B** ideally	**C** suitably	**D** appropriately
12	**A** surface	**B** land	**C** ground	**D** floor

Use of English • Part 2

For questions **13–24**, read the text below and think of the word which best fits each gap. Use only one word in each gap. There is an example at the beginning (**0**).

Write your answers **IN CAPITAL LETTERS on the separate answer sheet**.

Example: | **0** | T | O | | | | | | | | | | | | | | | | | | | |

The London Mini Marathon

Children come from all over Great Britain **(0)** .... take part in a mini marathon in London every

year. It is for children aged between 11 and 17 but, because it is such **(13)** .... popular event,

they have to be selected. Great Britain is divided **(14)** .... regions and team managers choose

(15) .... children will represent each region. After **(16)** .... selected, children are expected

to attend training sessions. There is also a wheelchair race but, for this race, the rule is that the

children **(17)** .... to be over 14. Teams consist **(18)** .... runners from three different

age groups and each age group has a slightly different start time **(19)** .... that they are

not all running at the same time. There is one thing about the London Mini Marathon that makes

(20) .... unique compared to other 'mini' races for kids. It is **(21)** .... only run on the

same day as the main London Marathon race for adults but it is also run on part of the same course.

This is **(22)** .... it is especially exciting for those chosen to **(23)** .... part in it. They run

along some of the most famous London streets, such **(24)** .... The Mall near Buckingham

Palace, where the Royal Family live.

Use of English • Part 3

For questions **25–34**, read the text below. Use the word given in capitals at the end of some of the lines to form a word that fits the gap in the same line. There is an example at the beginning (**0**).

Write your answers **IN CAPITAL LETTERS on the separate answer sheet**.

Example: | 0 | F | A | M | O | U | S | | | | | | | | | | | | | | | |

One man and his robots

Wu Yulu, who lives on the outskirts of Beijing, is **(0)** .... for	**FAME**
the robots he builds. In his **(25)** .... , people are used to	**NEIGHBOUR**
seeing him being pulled along in a cart by a robot which also has	
the **(26)** .... to jump, paint and drink, among other things.	**ABLE**
Wu Yulu's **(27)** .... with robots began when he was	**OBSESS**
a child. He would have liked to become an **(28)** .... but he	**ENGINE**
became a farmer instead. He made his first robot when he was	
11 but, **(29)** .... , it was unable to move. He continued to	**FORTUNE**
experiment, increasing his technical **(30)** .... until he finally	**KNOW**
managed to make one with arms and legs.	
Since then he has made over 40 robots and has been	
recognised worldwide for these **(31)** .... His aim is to	**INVENT**
make robots which can be of **(32)** .... to humans with the	**ASSIST**
(33) .... tasks they need to perform in their daily lives like	**PRACTICE**
chopping vegetables. His robots are like children to him and he	
gives each one his family name. It is also very **(34)** .... that	**HELP**
he gives them a name which indicates the order in which he built	
them.	

Use of English • Part 4

For questions **35–42**, complete the second sentence so that it has a similar meaning to the first sentence, using the word given. **Do not change the word given.** You must use between **two** and **five** words, including the word given. Here is an example (**0**).

Example:

0   There was such a big crowd waiting outside the stadium that I couldn't find my friends.

SO

There .... people waiting outside the stadium that I couldn't find my friends.

The gap can be filled by the words 'were so many', so you write:

Example: | **0** | WERE SO MANY |

Write **only** the missing words **IN CAPITAL LETTERS on the separate answer sheet**.

---

35   Despite having plenty of money, Josh decided not to buy the football boots.

EVEN

Josh decided not to buy the football boots .... plenty of money.

36   The dance class was cancelled because of a lack of interest among the students.

ENOUGH

The dance class was cancelled because not .... interested.

37   It's a pity I got there after the film had started.

WISH

I .... arrived after the film had started.

38   My teacher suggested that I should enter the drama competition.

WHY

My teacher said: '............................... enter the drama competition?'

39 I know I didn't leave my bag at school because I took my phone out on the bus.

CAN'T

I took my phone out on the bus so .... my bag at school.

40 My grandfather was 70 when he started running.

TAKE

My grandfather .... until he was 70.

41 We need to walk faster or the shops will be closed when we get there.

UNLESS

The shops will be closed when we get there .... faster.

42 Everyone will get a free drink at the beginning of the race.

GIVEN

Free drinks .... everyone at the beginning of the race.

Listening • Part 1

Questions 1–8

🔘 1.24 You will hear people talking in eight different situations. For questions **1–8**, choose the best answer (**A**, **B** or **C**).

1   You overhear two students discussing a TV programme they have just watched.

What did they both like about the programme?

    A   the main character
    B   the unusual plot
    C   the background music

2   You hear a boy telling a friend about a sailing course he has just done.

What is the boy's opinion of the course?

    A   It was more difficult than he expected.
    B   It was badly affected by the weather conditions.
    C   It was designed for very young students.

3   You hear a teacher telling her students about a project they are going to do.

What does she warn them about?

    A   using internet material
    B   making spelling mistakes
    C   writing too much

4   You hear a girl talking on the radio about her favourite band.

Why is she attracted to their songs?

    A   They sing about familiar things.
    B   They play unusual instruments.
    C   They come from her area.

5   You overhear two students talking about what happened in an art class at school.

What problem did the boy have in his class?

A   He chose the wrong person to draw.

B   He selected an unsuitable paint colour.

C   He spilled something on his drawing.

6   You overhear a girl talking on the phone about a shopping trip.

What pleased her about the trip?

A   She bought a dress for a special occasion.

B   She got a bargain in the sales.

C   She found a new shop she liked.

7   You overhear two students talking about a castle in Scotland.

What does the boy think the castle would be a good setting for?

A   a ghost film

B   a documentary

C   a children's story

8   You hear a sports presenter talking about a running race.

What does he say about the winner of the race?

A   She shouldn't have competed yesterday.

B   She has just recovered from injury.

C   She was ahead of the others from the start.

Listening • Part 2

Questions 9–18

🔘 1.25 You will hear a young chef called Tom Neilson talking about the cookery competition he has just won. For questions **9–18**, complete the sentences.

Young Chef Competition

The competition, which is arranged by a group of [_____ **9**], began ten years ago.

Tom says that teenagers compare top chefs to celebrities they see on [_____ **10**] .

Competitors only have to cook a [_____ **11**] for the first stage of the competition.

Tom thinks that calculating the precise [_____ **12**] of the meal you make in the local final is difficult.

In the local final you are also tested on various things such as [_____ **13**] in the kitchen.

A professional chef gives [_____ **14**] to the people who reach the regional finals.

In the regional finals, the [_____ **15**] you do for the meal is considered very important.

Tom feels that competing in the national final is challenging because the [_____ **16**] you have to work with are chosen for you.

In the national final you are assessed on the [_____ **17**] of your food as well as your cooking skills.

If you get first prize, you spend two weeks in the [_____ **18**] of a top chef.

Listening • Part 3

🔊 1.26 You will hear five people talking about school visits to places of interest. For questions **19–23**, choose from the list (**A–F**) what each speaker says. Use each letter only once. There is one extra letter which you do not need to use.

A I decided on a career during the visit.

Speaker 1 [ ] **19**

B I learnt a new skill during the visit.

Speaker 2 [ ] **20**

C I thought we had a good guide on the visit.

Speaker 3 [ ] **21**

D I changed my view of the past as a result of the visit.

Speaker 4 [ ] **22**

E I was surprised the visit was so interactive.

Speaker 5 [ ] **23**

F I used my scientific knowledge during the visit.

Listening • Part 4

Questions 24–30

🔘 1.27 You will hear an interview with an American girl who sings in a choir. For questions **24–30**, choose the best answer (**A**, **B** or **C**).

24 What does Gina say about the members of her choir?

   A They come from schools specialising in music.

   B They have previous experience of singing.

   C They have formal qualifications in music.

25 What has belonging to a choir enabled Gina to do?

   A change the way she sings

   B become more self-critical

   C gain confidence in herself

26 Gina feels that through mixing with people in the choir, she has learnt

   A how to understand different cultures.

   B how to make new friends.

   C how to get people to agree.

27 What is Gina's attitude to the music she sings?

   A She likes singing a wide range of songs.

   B She particularly enjoys performing jazz songs.

   C She appreciates being able to suggest songs for the choir.

28 What does Gina say about expressing emotion through music?

   A It is something anyone in the choir can do.

   B It is easier to express happiness than sadness.

   C It is hard to convey emotion to other people.

29 How does Gina feel about performing in public?

   A a little frightened

   B slightly stressed

   C ready to be criticised

30 According to Gina, what is the choir director's main strength?

   A his personality

   B his musical ability

   C his conducting skills

Speaking • Part 1

3 minutes (5 minutes for groups of three)

The interlocutor introduces themselves and asks the candidates their names as below:

> Good morning/afternoon/evening. My name is .... and this is my colleague ....
>
> And your names are?
>
> Can I have your mark sheets, please?
>
> First of all, we'd like to know something about you.
> - Where are you from, (Candidate A)?
> - And you, (Candidate B)?
> - What do you like about living (here/name of candidate's home town)?
> - And what about you, (Candidate A/B)?

The examiner will ask each of you questions about everyday life. Here are some example topics and questions:

Everyday life

- Do you live near the school? ..... (How do you get to school?)
- When do you usually do your homework?
- What things do you enjoy doing at home in the evening?
- Does your family have a meal together in the evening? ..... (What do you like to eat?)
- What are you going to do this weekend?

Holidays

- Where do you go if you go away in the school holidays?
- What do you like doing if you stay at home during the holidays?
- Do you spend more time with your family or friends in the holidays? ..... (What do you do?)
- Are there enough things to do in the area where you live?
- What do you think is the best thing about school holidays?

Speaking • Part 2

4 minutes (6 minutes for groups of three)

The examiner gives each of you two photographs and asks you to talk about your photographs on your own for about a minute and also to answer a short question about your partner's photographs.

> *(Candidate A)*, it's your turn first. Here are your photographs (page 123). They show **people doing different kinds of exercise**.
>
> I'd like you to compare the photographs, and say **what the benefits of doing these kinds of exercise are**.

When Student A has finished, the examiner asks Student B a question.

> *(Candidate B)*, **how do you keep fit?**

> Now, *(Candidate B)*, here are your photographs (page 124). They show **different kinds of birthday parties**.
>
> I'd like you to compare the photographs and say **what the advantages and disadvantages of these kinds of parties are**.

When Student B has finished, the examiner asks Student A a question.

> *(Candidate A)*, **how do you usually celebrate your birthday?**

Speaking • Parts 3 and 4

7 minutes (9 minutes for groups of three)

The examiner asks you to talk about something together for about three minutes *(4 minutes for groups of three)*.

> **Here are some things your school could spend some money on** (page 25).
> First, talk to each other about **which of these things would be useful for most students**.
> Then decide **which two you would choose not to spend the money on**.

In Part 4, the examiner asks you some questions related to the activity in Part 3. You talk together about your answers.

Here are some examples of questions you might have:
- **Some people say students spend too much time studying and not enough time doing other things. What do you think?**
- **Should schools provide sports facilities or should children do sport outside school?**
- **Do you think schools should have an orchestra? Why? / Why not?**
- **Which activities do you do outside school? Which do you enjoy the most?**
- **Do you think drama is an important subject to include at school? Why? / Why not?**
- **Some people say that practical subjects like design and technology and art are as important as academic subjects. What do you think?**

What are the benefits of doing these kinds of exercise?

What are the advantages and disadvantages of these kinds of birthday parties?

- Which of these facilities would be useful for most students?
- Which two would you choose not to spend money on?

Unit 2 Speaking Part 3

Unit 4 Speaking Part 3

Acknowledgements

Author acknowledgements
The authors would like to thank their editors, Ann-Marie Murphy and Diane Hall, for their expertise and constant support. Many thanks also to Linda Matthews (production controller), Michelle Simpson (permissions controller), Hilary Luckcock (picture researcher), Leon Chambers (audio producer), Marcus Fletcher (proof reader).

Publisher acknowledgements
The authors and publishers are grateful to the following for reviewing the material during the writing process:
Susan Obiglio: Argentina; Maria Christaki: Greece; Jane Hoatson, Jessica Smith, Catherine Toomey: Italy; Katherine Bilsborough, Laura Clyde: Spain; Ludmila Kozhevnikova: Russia; Bridget Bloom, Helen Chilton, Mark Fountain, Rebecca Raynes: UK.
Thanks are also due to the teachers who contributed to initial research in to this course. In Milan, Italy: Judith Axelby, Liane Hyde, Rachel Shields, Prof. Barbagallo, Prof. Marrali; in Turin: Prof. Cook, Prof. Dickens, Prof. Grasso, Prof. Zoppas; in Genova: Prof. Lovati, Prof. Risso. In Poland: teachers at Empik, Warsaw Study Centre, Warsaw University, ZS UMK. In Spain: Keith Appleby, Vicante Ferarios Maroto, Nick Tunstall, Lisa Wotton. In Switzerland: Keith Dabourn, Ms Eigner, Amy Jost, Ueli Hepp, Lori Kaithen, Eveline Reichel, Lee Walker and teachers at Berlitz, Berufschule Bulach, Sprachschule Schneiner, Liz and Michelle from the apprenticeship school.

Development of this publication has made use of the Cambridge English Corpus (CEC). The CEC is a computer database of contemporary spoken and written English, which currently stands at over one billion words. It includes British English, American English and other varieties of English. It also includes the Cambridge Learner Corpus, developed in collaboration with the University of Cambridge ESOL Examinations. Cambridge University Press has built up the CEC to provide evidence about language use that helps to produce better language teaching materials.

This product is informed by the English Vocabulary Profile, built as part of English Profile, a collaborative programme designed to enhance the learning, teaching and assessment of English worldwide. Its main funding partners are Cambridge University Press and Cambridge ESOL and its aim is to create a 'profile' for English linked to the Common European Framework of Reference for Languages (CEFR). English Profile outcomes, such as the English Vocabulary Profile, will provide detailed information about the language that learners can be expected to demonstrate at each CEFR level, offering a clear benchmark for learners' proficiency. For more information, please visit www.englishprofile.org.

Text acknowledgements
The authors and publishers acknowledge the following sources of copyright material and are grateful for the permissions granted. While every effort has been made, it has not always been possible to identify the sources of all the material used, or to trace all copyright holders. If any omissions are brought to our notice, we will be happy to include the appropriate acknowledgements on reprinting.

Robin's Nest Productions, Inc for the text on p. 10 adapted from *Hold on Tight* by Robin Gunn, Copyright © 1998 Robin Gunn. Reproduced with permission; DOGO Media, Inc for the text on p. 51 adapted from 'Even Humpback Whales release hit singles' by Meera Dolasia, DOGONews, 15/4/2011. Reproduced with permission; Random House Group Limited for the text on pp. 58-9 adapted from *The Tarot Reader's Daughter* by Helen Dunwoodie, published by Corgi Books. Reprinted by permission of The Random House Group Ltd; HarperCollins Publishers for the text on p. 102 adapted from pp. 3-8 from Bounce Copyright © 2010 Matthew Syed. Reprinted by permission of HarperCollins Publishers Ltd; Guardian News & Media Ltd for the text on p. 104 adapted from 'If dinosaurs weren't actually big, what else don't scientists know? By Paul Barrett, *The Guardian* 09/06/2012. Copyright © Guardian News & Media Ltd, 2012.

Photo acknowledgements
T = Top, C = Centre, B = Below, L = Left, R = Right, B/G = background

The publisher has used its best endeavours to ensure that the URLs for external websites referred to in this book are correct and active at the time of going to press. However, the publisher has no responsibility for the websites and can make no guarantee that a site will remain live or that the content is or will remain appropriate.

Header photos: Reading: istockphoto/artpipi; Speaking: istockphoto/drbimages; Listening: istockphoto/coloroftime; Grammar: istockphoto/ManuelBurgos; Writing: istockphoto/DNY59.
p. 6(T): Getty Images/Rob Lewine; p. 6(C): istockphoto/RonTech2000; p. 6(B): Corbis/Andersen Ross/Cultura; p. 7: Getty Images/Dominick Smitz; p. 9(TL): Thinkstock/David De Lossy; p. 9(C): Fotolia/Mr Markin; p. 9(TR): istockphoto/Alija; p. 9(BR): Thorpe Park; p.13: Getty Images/Konrad Wothe; p. 14(L): Fotolia/Gail Johnson; p. 14(C): Fotolia/MikiG; p. 14(R): Alamy/Stuart Pearce; p. 15: Getty Images/Ryan McVay; p. 16: Alamy/Mary Evans Picture Library; p. 17: Fotolia/erika palla; pp. 18/126(TL): Alamy/David L Moore; pp. 18/126(TC): Alamy/Alex Segre; pp. 18/126(TR): Alamy/Robert Stainforth; pp. 18/126(BL): Getty Images/AFP; pp. 18/126(BR): Alamy/David Levenson; p. 19(L): Alamy/Elizabeth Czitronyi; p. 19(B): Superstock/imagebroker.net; p. 19(R): Alamy/Peter Phipp/Travelshots.com; p. 22: Fotolia/Miravision; p. 23(T): The Kobal Collection/Lucasfilm/Paramount Pictures; p. 23(CT): Rex Features/Sony Pics/Everett; p. 23(CB): The Kobal Collection/Warner Bros/DC Comics; p. 23(B): Alamy/AF Archive; p. 24(T): The Kobal Collection/RP Films; p. 24(B): The Kobal Collection/Screen Gems; p. 26(T): Glowimages/Radius; p. 26(CR): Glowimages/Stockbroker; p. 26(CL): Alamy/Geoff du Feu; p. 26(B): Masterfile; p. 27(L): Getty Images/Nick Onken; p. 27(R): Superstock/Eye Ubiquitous; p. 28: Alamy/Hemis; p. 30(L): Alamy/Images-USA; p. 30(R): Glowimages/Aflo Score; p. 32(T): Thinkstock/istockphoto; p. 32(B): Getty Images/Robert Decelis Ltd; pp. 33/126(TL): Alamy/Steve Skjold; pp. 33/126(TC): Alamy/aberCPC; pp. 33/126(TR): Fotolia/Alen Ajan; pp. 33/126(BL): Masterfile; pp. 33/126(BC): Shutterstock/tankist 276; p. 33(BR): Corbis/Images Source; p. 34: Glowimages/Images; p. 35: Masterfile; p. 38(TL): Alamy/Ashley Cooper Pics; p. 38(TR): Glowimages/Cultura; p. 38(BL): Thinkstock/Digital Vision; p. 38(BR): Getty Images/DreamPictures; p. 39(T): Thinkstock/Comstock Images; p. 39(CT): Masterfile/Aflo Relax; p. 39(C): Thinkstock/istockphoto; 39(CB): Alamy/Rubberball; p. 39(C): Corbis/David Katzenstein/Citizenstock; p. 42: Alamy/Greg Balfour Evans; p. 43(T,B): Aeroseum, Sweden; p. 44(TL): Corbis/moodboard; p. 44(TR): Alamy/MBI; p. 44(BL): Alamy/El Chapulin; p. 44(BR): Alamy/Chris Cooper-Smith; p. 46(TL): Superstock/Minden Pictures; p. 46(TC): Alamy/Philip Mugridge; p. 46(TR): Superstock/Michael Wheatley/All Canada Photos; p. 46(B): Alamy/Greatstock Photographic Library; p. 50(L): Glowimages/Wolfgang Kaehler; p. 50(C): Shutterstock/Stu Porter; p. 50(TR): istockphoto/Jim Parkin; p. 54(T): Alamy/Rubberball; p. 54(C): Alamy/dov makabaw; p. 54(B): Alamy/John Powell-Photographer; p. 56(T): Getty Images/Picturenet; p. 56(CT): Alamy/Justin Kase z08z; p. 56(CB): Alamy/David J Green-Lifestyle themes; p. 56(B): Superstock/ICP/age fotostock; p. 62(T): Alamy/Martin Shields; p. 62(C): Fotolia/auremar; p. 62(B): Masterfile; p. 63(TL): Masterfile/Rick Gomez; p. 63(BL): Alamy/Catchlight Visual Services; p. 63(TR): Thinkstock/istockphoto; p. 63(BR): Glowimages/GogoImages; p. 65: Alamy/WILDLIFE GmbH; p. 67: Rex Features/Geoffrey Robinson; pp. 68/127(TV): Thinkstock/Jupiterimages; pp. 68/127(laptop): Shutterstock/EDHAR; pp. 68/127(smartphone): istockphoto/gianlucabartoli; pp. 68/127(fridge-freezer): Fotolia/Piotr Pawinski; pp. 68/127(luxury car): istockphoto/Trevor Smith; pp. 68/127(mountain bike): Shutterstock/hamurishi; pp. 68/127(digital camera): Thinkstock/Tony Cordoza; p. 71: Corbis/Ocean; p. 74: Alamy/AfriPics.com; p. 77(Science Photo Library/Emilio Segre Visual Archives/American Institute of Physics; p. 80: Corbis/Joe Stevens/Retna Ltd; p. 90: Alamy/Picture Press; p. 102: Glowimages/Image Source; p. 104: Alamy/leonello calvetti; p. 107(TL): Shutterstock/Tracy Whiteside; p. 107(CL): Fotolia/RTW 590; p. 107(TR): Thinkstock/Pixland; p. 107(CR): istockphoto/Trevor Smith; p. 107(BR): Thinkstock/Huntstock; p. 112: Virgin Money Giving Mini London Marathon; p. 121: Trevor Clifford; p. 123(T): Shutterstock/Denis Kuvaev; p. 123(B): Alamy/David Young-Wolff; p. 124(T): Thinkstock/Comstock Images; p. 124(B): Alamy/Bubbles Photolibrary.

Picture Research: Hilary Luckcock.

Illustrations by:
John Batten (Beehive Illustration) pp.20, 27, 121, 125;
Maxwell Dorsley (New Division) pp.52, 53, 79, 80, 82, 85, 86, 88;
Richard Jones (Beehive Illustration) pp.10, 11, 40, 42;
Kate Rochester (Pickled Ink) pp.25, 30, 35, 36, 73;
Laszlo Veres (Beehive Illustration) pp.8, 22, 48, 58, 60;

Design, layout and art edited by: Wild Apple Design Ltd.